Beekeeping For Beginners

Master Bee Care from Site Selection to Honey Extraction | Includes Bonus: DIY Lush Cologne with a Definitive Step-by-Step Guide

Thaddeus Hivesworth

© Copyright 2023 - All rights reserved.
The content contained within this book may not be reproduced, duplicated, or transmitted without direct written permission from the author or the publisher.

Under no circumstances will any blame or legal responsibility be held against the publisher, or author, for any damages, reparation, or monetary loss due to the information contained within this book. Either directly or indirectly.

Legal Notice:

This book is copyright protected. This book is only for personal use. You cannot amend, distribute, sell, use, quote, or paraphrase any part, or the content within this book, without the consent of the author or publisher.

Disclaimer Notice:

By reading this document, the reader agrees that under no circumstances is the author responsible for any losses, direct or indirect, which are incurred as a result of the use of the information contained within this document, including, but not limited to, - errors, omissions, or inaccuracies.

The information contained in this book and its contents is not designed to replace or take the place of any form of medical or professional advice; and is not meant to replace the need for independent medical, financial, legal or other professional advice or services, as may be required. The content and information in this book have been provided for educational and entertainment purposes only.

Table Of Contents

INTRODUCTION 6

CHAPTER 1: GETTING STARTED WITH BEEKEEPING 7
- Why Beekeeping? 7
- Beekeeping Benefits 8
- Preparations for Beekeeping 9

CHAPTER 2: UNDERSTANDING BEE ANATOMY AND BEHAVIOR 11
- The Anatomy of a Bee 11
- Life Inside the Beehive 11
- Behavioral Patterns 12
- The Importance of Observation 12
- Safety Precautions 13

CHAPTER 3: CHOOSING THE RIGHT BEEHIVE 14
- Types of Beehives 14

CHAPTER 4: OBTAINING AND INSTALLING YOUR FIRST BEES 17
- Obtaining Bees 17
- Preparing for Bee Arrival 18
- Installing Your Bees 18
- Monitoring and Early Care 19
- Common Challenges and Troubleshooting 19

CHAPTER 5: BEEHIVE MANAGEMENT BASICS 20
- Hive Inspections 20
- Handling Bees Safely 20
- Seasonal Hive Management 21
- Hive Health and Hygiene 21
- Swarm Prevention and Management 21
- Feeding Your Bees Feeding Your Bees 22
- Queen Management 22
- Honey Extraction 23
- Record Keeping 23
- Sustainable Beekeeping Practices 24

CHAPTER 6: HIVE INSPECTIONS AND MAINTENANCE 25
- The Frequency of Inspections 25
- Tools and Equipment 26
- Preparing for an Inspection 27
- The Hive Inspection Process 28
- Recognizing and Addressing Issues 28
- Hive Hygiene 29
- Record Keeping and Documentation 29
- Beekeeping Ethics 29

CHAPTER 7: COLLECTING HONEY AND HIVE PRODUCTS 31

- The Honey Harvesting Process 31
- Harvesting Tools and Equipment 31
- Extracting Honey 32
- Processing Beeswax 32
- Harvesting Propolis 32
- Royal Jelly Extraction 33
- Beehive Products Management 33
- Ethical Harvesting 33

CHAPTER 8: DEALING WITH COMMON BEEKEEPING CHALLENGES 34

- Pests and Parasites 34
- Diseases 34
- Robbing and Predation 35
- Swarming 35
- Queen Issues 35
- Environmental Factors 36
- Seasonal Management 36

CHAPTER 9: BEEKEEPING SEASONS AND ANNUAL HIVE CARE 38

- Spring: The Season of Renewal 38
- Summer: The Season of Abundance 38
- Fall: The Season of Preparation 38
- Winter: The Season of Rest 38
- Annual Hive Care 39

CHAPTER 10: EXPANDING YOUR BEEKEEPING OPERATION 40

- Increasing Hive Count 40
- Producing Nucleus Colonies 40
- Queen Rearing and Breeding 40
- Honey and Hive Product Sales 40
- Pollination Services 40
- Beekeeping Education 41
- Diversifying Hive Products 41
- Sustainable Practices in Expansion 41

CHAPTER 11: BEE HEALTH AND DISEASE MANAGEMENT 42

- Monitoring Bee Health 42
- Common Bee Diseases 42
- Prevention and Biosecurity 44
- Varroa Mites 44
- Small Hive Beetles and Wax Moths 44
- Integrated Pest Management (IPM) 44
- Treatment-Free Beekeeping 45
- Biosecurity and Preventive Measures 46

CHAPTER 12: BEEKEEPING AND ENVIRONMENTAL CONSERVATION 47

- The Importance of Bees in Ecosystems 47
- Pesticide Awareness 47
- Forage and Habitat Enhancement 47
- Avoiding Invasive Plants 47
- Reducing Environmental Footprint 47
- Participating in Citizen Science 48
- Promoting Pollinator-Friendly Policies 48

- Educating Others 48
- Supporting Native Bees 48

CHAPTER 13: BEEKEEPING CHALLENGES AND ADAPTATION 49
- Climate Change 49
- Pesticide Exposure 49
- Bee Health Issues 49
- Market Changes 49
- Regulatory Changes 50
- Technology and Innovation 50
- Community and Collaboration 53

CHAPTER 14: BEEKEEPING AND THE FUTURE 54
- Technological Advancements 54
- Urban Beekeeping 54
- Pollinator Health Initiatives 55
- Bee-Friendly Agriculture 55
- Research and Education 56
- Market Trends 56
- Global Collaboration 56

CHAPTER 15: YOUR BEEKEEPING LEGACY 57
- Beekeeping as a Lifelong Journey 57
- Passing on Knowledge 57
- Promoting Bee Health 57
- Supporting Local Pollinators 58
- Advocacy and Conservation 58
- Community Building 58
- Sustainable Practices 59
- Inspiring Others 59

CHAPTER BONUS: INTRODUCTION TO DIY BEEHIVE CONSTRUCTION 60
- Section 1 - Safety First 60
- Section 2: Gather Your Materials 61
- Section 3 - Choose Your Hive Design 63

CHAPTER BONUS 2: CONSTRUCTING HIVE BODIES 66
- Section 1 - Understanding Hive Bodies 66
- Section 2 - Gathering Your Materials 66
- Section 3 - Hive Body Assembly 67
- Section 4 - Preparing the Work Area 70
- Section 5 - Understanding Hive Components 72

CONCLUSION 74

INTRODUCTION

Welcome to the fascinating world of beekeeping! Whether you're a nature enthusiast, a budding entrepreneur, or simply someone who appreciates the importance of bees in our ecosystem, this comprehensive guide is designed to be your roadmap to successful beekeeping. Bees are not only vital pollinators for plants, but they also produce delicious honey and other valuable hive products. With the right knowledge and dedication, beekeeping can be a rewarding and sustainable endeavor.

In "Beekeeping for Beginners," we will take you on a journey from the very basics of beekeeping to advanced techniques and practices. From understanding the inner workings of a beehive to managing your colony, harvesting honey, and even exploring the commercial aspects of beekeeping, we will cover it all. By the end of this book, you will have the knowledge and confidence to embark on your beekeeping adventure.

Chapter 1: Getting Started with Beekeeping

Beekeeping is a fulfilling and eco-friendly hobby or business that anyone can embark upon. In this first chapter, we'll cover the foundational aspects of beekeeping, including why you should consider beekeeping, the benefits it offers, and the preparations you need to make before diving into this exciting endeavor.

Why Beekeeping?

Beekeeping is an age-old practice that has transcended the realms of agriculture and found a place in the hearts and lives of individuals worldwide. It is a craft that marries tradition with modernity, offering myriad reasons for both novices and experienced practitioners to embrace its enchanting world. But why beekeeping? What is it about this ancient art that continues to captivate the imaginations of people from all walks of life?

First and foremost, beekeeping is a captivating journey into the heart of one of nature's most intricate and harmonious societies: the honeybee colony. It provides an unparalleled opportunity to witness the remarkable lives of these tiny creatures, who, through their tireless work and collaboration, create not only the golden nectar we call honey but also pollinate the crops that sustain our food supply. The awe-inspiring complexity of a hive, with its caste system, intricate dances, and hive mind, reveals the genius of nature in its purest form.

Beyond the awe factor, beekeeping offers a profound sense of connection to the natural world. It compels beekeepers to become attuned to the rhythms of the seasons, the ebb and flow of nectar sources, and the subtle cues of their bee colonies. In a world increasingly dominated by screens and concrete, beekeeping provides a tangible link to the earth, reminding us of our place in the greater web of life.

Practicality is another compelling reason to embrace beekeeping. Beekeepers are rewarded with the fruits of their labor in the form of honey, beeswax, propolis, and other hive products. Honey, often referred to as "liquid gold," is not only a delectable natural sweetener but also a source of medicinal and culinary delight. Beeswax can be transformed into candles, cosmetics, and crafts, while propolis holds therapeutic properties that have been revered for centuries.

Moreover, beekeeping offers an avenue for sustainability and conservation. As pollinators, bees are vital to the reproduction of countless plant species, including many of our food crops. By tending to bee colonies, beekeepers play a pivotal role in the preservation of these crucial pollinators and the biodiversity of our ecosystems.

In conclusion, beekeeping is a multifaceted pursuit that captivates, educates, nourishes, and connects. It is an invitation to step into the enchanting world of honeybees, a reminder of our profound relationship with the natural world, and a practical endeavor with tangible rewards. For those who heed the call of the hive, beekeeping offers a journey filled with wonder, purpose, and the sweetest of pleasures.

Beekeeping Benefits

Beekeeping, often regarded as a niche hobby or agricultural pursuit, offers a plethora of benefits that extend far beyond the confines of a beehive. These advantages touch upon various aspects of human life, the environment, and the broader ecosystem, making beekeeping a truly enriching endeavor.

First and foremost, beekeeping provides a source of pure, natural, and locally-produced honey. This golden elixir not only delights the palate but also boasts an array of health benefits. Rich in antioxidants, vitamins, and enzymes, honey serves as a healthier alternative to refined sugars and can be used for culinary and medicinal purposes. Moreover, honey contains allergens from local plants, potentially aiding in the reduction of seasonal allergies for those who consume it regularly. Beekeeping contributes to the preservation of the environment by supporting pollinators.

Honeybees, as diligent pollinators, play a pivotal role in the reproduction of fruits, vegetables, and flowers. Their efforts result in improved crop yields and the biodiversity of ecosystems. Beekeeping, therefore, aligns with sustainable agriculture practices, promoting food security and ecological balance.

The benefits of beekeeping extend to personal well-being as well. Beekeepers often speak of the therapeutic and meditative qualities of tending to their colonies. The act of inspecting hives, handling bees, and observing their intricate social structure can be a calming and fulfilling experience. Beekeeping encourages mindfulness and a connection to the natural world, offering respite from the hustle and bustle of modern life.

Additionally, beekeeping fosters a sense of community and knowledge sharing. Beekeepers often come together to exchange ideas, advice, and experiences, forming networks that support both novice and seasoned enthusiasts. This sense of camaraderie and collective learning enhances the beekeeping journey.

Preparations for Beekeeping

To set yourself up for success, you'll need to make several preparations before getting your first beehive. We'll discuss the legal and regulatory aspects of beekeeping in your area, as well as the equipment and protective gear you'll need. Additionally, you'll learn about the importance of choosing the right location for your hive and creating a safe and supportive environment for your future bee colony.

Below, we outline essential steps and considerations for your preparations:

1. Educate Yourself: Before getting your first hive, invest time in learning about beekeeping. Books, online resources, beekeeping courses, and local beekeeping associations are valuable sources of knowledge. Understanding the biology and behavior of honeybees is fundamental.
2. Choose Your Hive Type: Select the type of beehive that suits your goals and resources. Common options include Langstroth hives, top-bar hives, and Warre hives. Each has its advantages and disadvantages, so choose one that aligns with your beekeeping objectives.
3. Locate a Suitable Apiary Site: Find a suitable location for your apiary. It should provide ample forage for bees, protection from strong winds, access to water, and adequate sunlight. Ensure that local regulations and neighbors allow for beekeeping.
4. Obtain the Necessary Equipment: Invest in essential beekeeping equipment, including protective gear (bee suit, veil, gloves), hive tools, a smoker, and the chosen type of beehive. Having the right tools is crucial for safe and effective hive management.
5. Source Your Bees: Acquire a package of bees or a nucleus colony (nuc) from a reputable source. Bees can be ordered from beekeepers or apiaries. Ensure they come from a healthy and disease-free source.
6. Assemble and Prepare Your Hive: Assemble your beehive according to the manufacturer's instructions. Ensure it is well-ventilated, stable, and positioned on a level surface. Prepare frames with foundation or starter strips for the bees to build comb.
7. Familiarize Yourself with Bee Health and Disease Management: Learn about common bee diseases and pests, as well as management strategies. Being proactive in disease prevention is vital for the long-term health of your colony.
8. Develop a Feeding Plan: Depending on your location and the time of year you start beekeeping, you may need to provide supplemental food to your bees until they can forage for nectar and pollen.

9. Create a Beekeeping Schedule: Develop a schedule for hive inspections, which vary depending on the season. Regular inspections help you monitor the health of your colony, assess their food stores, and detect any issues early.

10. Safety Measures: Always prioritize safety when working with bees. Have a plan for handling stings and ensure that someone knows about your beekeeping activities in case of emergencies.

11. Local Regulations and Permits: Check with local authorities or beekeeping associations for any regulations or permits required for keeping bees in your area. Compliance with local laws is essential.

12. Join a Beekeeping Association: Consider joining a local beekeeping association or club. These organizations provide valuable support, mentorship, and opportunities to connect with experienced beekeepers.

Preparations for beekeeping demand dedication, patience, and a willingness to continue learning. With the right knowledge and equipment, you'll be well on your way to a rewarding and sustainable beekeeping experience.

Chapter 2: Understanding Bee Anatomy and Behavior

In this chapter, we will delve deeper into the world of bees, exploring their intricate anatomy and behavior. Understanding the inner workings of a bee is crucial for effective beekeeping, as it allows you to anticipate their needs and respond to their behaviors appropriately.

The Anatomy of a Bee

The intricate and finely tuned body of a honeybee is a masterpiece of nature, designed for the precise functions required for its role in the hive and as a pollinator of flowering plants. To understand the world of bees fully, one must delve into the fascinating anatomy of these remarkable insects.

At first glance, a bee may appear simple, but a closer examination reveals a highly specialized and complex structure. Bees are divided into three main body parts: the head, thorax, and abdomen. The head houses the sensory organs, including compound eyes for detecting light and movement, and antennae for touch, taste, and smell. The mandibles, strong jaws, are used for various tasks within the hive.

Attached to the thorax are three pairs of legs and two pairs of wings. The legs are equipped with an array of bristles and specialized structures for grooming, collecting pollen, and manipulating food. The wings, a marvel of aerodynamic engineering, enable bees to perform intricate flight patterns while foraging for nectar and pollen.

The abdomen, perhaps the most vital part, houses the bee's digestive and reproductive systems. It is also the location of the wax glands used to construct comb and the stinger for defense. The abdomen is divided into segments, each with specific functions related to digestion, respiration, and reproduction.

Remarkably, within this compact and efficient body, bees carry out a myriad of tasks essential for the survival of the colony. They navigate through complex environments, communicate through intricate dances, and perform precise tasks with their specialized body parts. Understanding the anatomy of a bee is not only a glimpse into the wonders of the natural world but also a key to unlocking the mysteries of bee behavior and the intricate workings of the hive. It is a testament to the evolutionary perfection of these tiny insects, which play an outsized role in shaping our ecosystems and providing for our sustenance through pollination.

Life Inside the Beehive

Within the confines of a beehive lies a bustling metropolis teeming with purpose and cooperation. The bee colony operates as a superorganism, with every member playing a crucial role. At its heart is the queen bee, the mother of the colony, laying thousands of eggs each day. Worker bees, the majority of the population, assume various tasks, from nursing and foraging to building and defending the hive. These diligent workers communicate through intricate dances to share information about the location of nectar sources. Drones, the male bees, have a simpler role – to mate with the queen. The hive's organization, hygiene, and temperature regulation are awe-inspiring feats of collective effort. Life inside the beehive is a testament to the power of cooperation and instinct, where each individual's actions contribute to the survival and success of the colony.

Behavioral Patterns

The behavioral patterns of bees are a testament to the remarkable coordination and intelligence within a hive. Bees exhibit intricate and highly specialized behaviors that ensure the colony's survival and productivity. One of the most famous examples is the waggle dance, a complex communication system used by forager bees to convey information about the location of food sources. Bees also demonstrate remarkable division of labor, with worker bees transitioning through different roles as they age, from nursing larvae to guarding the hive or foraging for nectar and pollen. Additionally, bees are known for their hygiene and cleanliness, regularly cleaning their hive to prevent disease. These behavioral patterns are not merely instinctual but also responsive to the colony's changing needs, a testament to the sophisticated social organization of honeybee colonies.

The Importance of Observation

Observation is the cornerstone of successful beekeeping, a practice that hinges on understanding the complex world of honeybees. Beekeepers keenly observe their hives to assess the health, behavior, and needs of their colonies. Through attentive monitoring, they can detect early signs of disease, pest infestations, or issues with the queen. Observation also extends to the surrounding environment, where beekeepers track flowering patterns and weather conditions that affect foraging.
Furthermore, observation is a key tool for learning about bee behavior, from the waggle dances that convey foraging information to the intricacies of swarm preparations. It fosters a deep connection with the bees and their ecosystem. In beekeeping, the art of observation is a skill honed over time, a vital link between the beekeeper and their bees, enabling responsible stewardship and the well-being of these remarkable insects.

Safety Precautions

Beekeeping is a rewarding endeavor, but it comes with inherent risks, primarily associated with bee stings and potential allergic reactions. Thus, safety precautions are paramount.

Protective gear is a beekeeper's first line of defense. This includes a bee suit, veil, gloves, and closed-toe shoes. The goal is to minimize exposed skin and prevent bee stings.

A well-lit, calm, and smoke-fueled environment during hive inspections helps keep bees docile. Additionally, working slowly and deliberately reduces the likelihood of provoking defensive behaviors.

Regular self-assessment for allergies or sensitivities to bee stings is vital. Having an emergency plan, including an EpiPen and knowledge of its use, can be lifesaving.

Lastly, beekeepers should share their activities with someone aware of their location and schedule in case of emergencies.

Safety precautions ensure that the joys of beekeeping are accompanied by responsible practices that prioritize both the beekeeper's well-being and the health of the bee colony.

Chapter 3: Choosing the Right Beehive

Selecting the right beehive is a pivotal decision in beekeeping, one that reverberates throughout your entire journey. The beehive serves as the epicenter of your bee colony's world, impacting their well-being and productivity. In this chapter, we embark on a journey to explore the diverse options available to beekeepers, each hive type with its unique advantages and characteristics. The choice between Langstroth hives, top-bar hives, Warre hives, or other alternatives is not merely a matter of aesthetics; it aligns with your beekeeping objectives, resources, and philosophy. Your hive selection influences hive management, honey production, and even the ease of inspections. As we delve into the details, you'll gain insight into the practical and philosophical considerations guiding your choice, empowering you to make an informed decision that resonates with your vision as a beekeeper.

Types of Beehives

In the world of beekeeping, the choice of beehive type is a decision that reverberates throughout your beekeeping journey. Each hive design offers unique advantages and considerations, allowing beekeepers to tailor their approach to their goals and preferences. Here are some of the most common types of beehives:

- **Langstroth Hives:**

  Langstroth hives are the workhorses of modern beekeeping, offering a standardized and highly efficient design. They feature removable frames suspended in stackable boxes, allowing for easy inspection and honey extraction. The versatility of Langstroth hives makes them suitable for various beekeeping goals, from honey production to pollination services. Beekeepers appreciate the ability to expand vertically, providing ample space for bee colonies to thrive. The Langstroth hive's uniform frame sizes enable compatibility with commercial beekeeping accessories, simplifying hive management. While they require a degree of intervention, Langstroth hives are favored for their high honey yields and adaptability, making them a common choice for both novice and experienced beekeepers.

- **Top-Bar Hives:**

  Top-bar hives offer a departure from the standardized frame systems of Langstroth hives, emphasizing a more naturalistic approach to beekeeping. In these hives, bees build their comb suspended from horizontal bars, allowing for flexibility and minimal disruption during inspections. Top-bar hives are favored by beekeepers who prioritize a hands-off, bee-friendly philosophy. They are particularly well-suited for smaller-scale beekeeping and those interested in sustainable and natural beekeeping practices. While top-bar hives may yield less honey compared to Langstroth hives, their appeal lies in their simplicity, affordability, and the minimal stress they impose on bee colonies, making them an excellent choice for those who value a closer connection to the bees and their natural behaviors.

- **Warre Hives:**

Warre hives, named after their creator Emile Warre, are designed with a strong focus on replicating the natural behaviors of bees. These hives emphasize vertical expansion, allowing bees to build their comb and move upward. They promote minimal intervention, as beekeepers add new boxes to the bottom, encouraging bees to move upward as they naturally do in the wild. Warre hives are appreciated for their bee-centric approach, prioritizing colony health and minimal stress. While honey production may be slightly lower compared to Langstroth hives, the beekeeper's role is more hands-off, aligning with a natural and sustainable beekeeping philosophy. Warre hives are a favorite among those who seek a more holistic and bee-friendly approach to beekeeping.

- **Flow Hives:**

Flow hives represent a relatively recent innovation in beekeeping, designed to simplify the honey harvesting process. They feature a unique mechanism that allows beekeepers to extract honey without disturbing the hive or opening the individual frames. With the turn of a key, honey flows from the frames directly into a collection jar, significantly reducing the stress on the bees during harvest. This innovation is especially appealing to beekeepers seeking convenience and minimal disruption to the colony. While flow hives come with a higher initial investment, their ease of use and reduced intrusion make them popular among those looking for a user-friendly approach to beekeeping and honey extraction.

- **Horizontal Hives:**

Horizontal hives, exemplified by designs like the Kenyan top-bar hive, offer a unique alternative to the vertical stack of Langstroth hives. In horizontal hives, frames or bars run parallel to the ground, encouraging bees to build comb along a horizontal plane. This approach mimics the bees' natural tendencies and fosters a more organic, low-intervention beekeeping style. These hives are often favored in warmer climates and for smaller-scale beekeeping operations. While horizontal hives may yield less honey compared to vertical designs, their appeal lies in simplicity, sustainability, and alignment with a bee-friendly philosophy that seeks to minimize disruption and support the bees in their natural behaviors.

Chapter 4: Obtaining and Installing Your First Bees

Now that you've chosen the right beehive, it's time to take the next step in your beekeeping journey: acquiring your first colony of bees and introducing them to their new home. In this chapter, we'll guide you through the process of obtaining bees, whether through purchasing a package, capturing a swarm, or acquiring a nucleus colony. We'll also cover the crucial steps for safely installing your bees in their new hive.

Obtaining Bees

Before you can start beekeeping, you need bees to populate your hive. There are several ways to obtain bees, each with its advantages and considerations:

1. **Package Bees** Package bees are a common means of starting a new colony in beekeeping. These packages typically consist of thousands of worker bees, a queen, and a sugar syrup or fondant food source. Beekeepers purchase package bees, often in screened boxes, and transfer them to their own hives. This method offers several advantages, including the ability to introduce a new colony or replace a declining one. It's a convenient way for beekeepers to obtain bees, especially when local bee breeders may not be available. However, package bees require careful handling during installation to ensure the acceptance and establishment of the new colony, making it an essential skill for beekeepers.

2. **Nucleus Colonies (Nucs)**: Nucleus colonies, often referred to as "nucs," are small, self-contained bee colonies created from a larger, established hive. A nuc typically consists of a queen, several frames of brood (young bees in various developmental stages), worker bees, and food stores. These mini-colonies are valuable assets for beekeepers, serving various purposes. Nucs can be used to create new colonies, replace queens in existing hives, or serve as a source of bees and queens for sale. They provide a head start for beekeepers, offering a ready-made, functional unit that can quickly grow into a productive hive. Nucleus colonies are a valuable tool in beekeeping for colony management, expansion, and genetic diversity.

3. **Capturing a Swarm**: Capturing a swarm is an exhilarating aspect of beekeeping. Swarms are nature's way of propagating honeybee colonies, and they occur when a colony

outgrows its hive and a portion of the bees, led by a new queen, departs to find a new home. Beekeepers can capture these swarms by providing a suitable hive or bait box. Once captured, the swarm can be hived, becoming a valuable addition to the beekeeper's apiary. Swarm capture not only increases the number of hives but also offers genetic diversity and a chance to help save feral honeybee populations.

Preparing for Bee Arrival

Before your bees arrive, it's essential to have everything in place. We'll cover the preparations you need to make, including ensuring your hive is set up correctly, having the necessary equipment on hand, and ensuring a suitable location for your hive.

Installing Your Bees

The process of introducing bees to their new home requires care and precision to minimize stress and ensure a smooth transition. We'll walk you through the steps of installing your bees, which typically involve:

1. **Smoking the Hive**:

   Smoking the hive is a crucial technique in beekeeping. Beekeepers use a smoker, which emits cool, white smoke, to calm and manage honeybees during hive inspections. The smoke triggers a natural response in the bees, encouraging them to consume honey and become less aggressive. This allows beekeepers to work in the hive with reduced risk of stings and minimal disruption to the colony. Proper smoke application is an essential skill, as it ensures a smoother and more productive inspection while prioritizing the well-being of both bees and beekeepers.

2. **Opening the Package or Nuc**:

   When beekeepers receive a package of bees or a nucleus colony (nuc), a carefully executed process is essential for their successful introduction to a new hive. This involves gently opening the package or nuc, releasing the bees into their new home, and ensuring the queen is safely introduced. Beekeepers need to work delicately, minimizing stress to the bees and ensuring they are comfortable and can quickly adapt to their new environment. Proper handling and attention to detail during this crucial step help establish a thriving colony in the beekeeper's apiary.

3. **Releasing the Queen**:

Releasing the queen bee into a new hive is a momentous event in beekeeping. After introducing a queen to her colony, she is often kept in a separate cage for a brief period. During this time, the worker bees become accustomed to her pheromones and accept her as their leader. The process of releasing the queen involves carefully removing the cage's plug, allowing the colony access to their new monarch. Timing and a gentle touch are crucial to ensure a smooth transition, promoting harmony and productivity within the hive. The successful release of the queen is a pivotal milestone in colony establishment and management.

4. **Feeding Your Bees**:

Beekeeping involves a vital aspect: ensuring your bees have an adequate food supply. This is particularly important during times of scarcity, such as early spring or late fall when natural forage may be limited. Beekeepers provide supplementary feed, often in the form of sugar syrup or fondant, to sustain their colonies. Feeding is a delicate balancing act, ensuring that the bees have enough sustenance to thrive without overfeeding, which can lead to issues like swarming or reduced honey production. Proper feeding supports the well-being of the colony, helping it weather periods of scarcity and flourish.

Monitoring and Early Care

Vigilant monitoring of bee colonies is a cornerstone of successful beekeeping. Regular hive inspections, typically conducted every 7-10 days during the active season, allow beekeepers to assess the colony's health, queen status, brood patterns, and food stores. Early detection of issues like disease, pests, or dwindling food supplies enables prompt intervention, preventing potential colony collapse. Adjustments in hive management, such as adding supers for honey storage or implementing pest control measures, can be implemented in response to observed needs. Monitoring and early care are critical for fostering thriving, resilient bee colonies and ensuring the sustainability of a beekeeper's apiary.

Common Challenges and Troubleshooting

Beekeepers often encounter various challenges while tending to their colonies. Common issues include the presence of pests like varroa mites, diseases such as American foulbrood, or queen problems like a failing or absent queen. Beekeepers need to be skilled troubleshooters, identifying these challenges through hive inspections and observations. Solutions may involve treatments, such as mite control methods, hive hygiene practices, or requeening. Timely and effective troubleshooting is vital to maintaining healthy colonies and preventing the spread of issues to neighboring hives, ensuring the overall well-being and productivity of the apiary.

Chapter 5: Beehive Management Basics

Now that you've successfully installed your first colony of bees, it's time to delve into the essential aspects of beekeeping management. In this chapter, we will cover the fundamental tasks and routines required to ensure the well-being and productivity of your bee colony.

Hive Inspections

Regular hive inspections are the backbone of conscientious beekeeping. During inspections, beekeepers carefully examine their colonies, assessing the health, behavior, and needs of the bees. These inspections involve opening the hive, removing frames, and observing the presence of the queen, brood patterns, and food stores. Beekeepers also look for signs of disease, pests, or other issues requiring attention. Proper hive inspections are a proactive measure, enabling early detection of problems and allowing for timely interventions to ensure colony health and productivity. They are a vital skill for beekeepers, promoting responsible stewardship and the well-being of their bee colonies.

Handling Bees Safely

Safety is paramount in beekeeping, and the art of handling bees safely is a core skill for beekeepers. It begins with wearing appropriate protective gear, including a bee suit, veil, gloves, and closed-toe shoes, which minimizes exposed skin and reduces the risk of stings. Approaching hives calmly, using a smoker to calm the bees, and working slowly and deliberately further minimize agitation. Beekeepers should also be aware of their own physical condition, as certain medications or allergies can increase sensitivity to bee stings.

Handling bees safely not only protects the beekeeper but also reduces stress on the colony, ensuring productive hive inspections and fostering a harmonious relationship between beekeepers and their bees.

Seasonal Hive Management

Effective beekeeping relies heavily on seasonal hive management, a dynamic approach that adapts to the changing needs of bee colonies throughout the year. Spring marks the start of increased colony activity, as bees forage for nectar and pollen. Beekeepers use this time for hive inspections, monitoring queen health, and adding supers to accommodate honey production. Summer brings a peak in foraging and honey storage, demanding vigilance against pests and swarming. Fall involves honey extraction, feeding bees for the winter, and preparing colonies for colder weather. Winter is a period of reduced activity, demanding minimal intervention but attention to insulation and food stores. Adapting to these seasonal shifts ensures thriving, resilient bee colonies and a successful beekeeping journey.

Hive Health and Hygiene

Maintaining hive health and hygiene is a fundamental responsibility for beekeepers. A clean and disease-free hive is essential for the well-being of bee colonies. Regular hive inspections are key to monitoring for signs of disease, pests, and other issues. Timely detection allows for swift intervention, preventing the spread of problems.

Hygiene within the hive is equally vital. Bees maintain impeccable cleanliness, regularly removing debris, dead bees, and larvae from the hive. Beekeepers can support this behavior by ensuring clean equipment and hive components.

Proper ventilation and hive spacing prevent moisture buildup, which can lead to fungal growth and stress on the colony. Adequate food stores are crucial, especially during winter months, to prevent starvation.

Promoting hive health and hygiene safeguards the productivity of the colony, minimizes disease transmission, and contributes to the sustainability of beekeeping operations. It reflects responsible beekeeping and a commitment to the well-being of these remarkable pollinators.

Swarm Prevention and Management

Swarming is a natural behavior in honeybee colonies, but beekeepers aim to manage and control it to prevent the loss of valuable bees and to maintain hive productivity. Swarm prevention involves strategies like providing ample space for bees to expand, regular inspections to detect queen cells, and splitting colonies before swarming impulses take hold.

In cases where swarming is imminent, swarm management techniques include capturing and rehiving the swarm, requeening, or dividing the colony. Beekeepers must understand swarm triggers, such as overcrowding or queen issues, and take proactive measures to address them. Effective swarm prevention and management are essential for maintaining colony strength and maximizing honey production in a responsible and sustainable manner.

Feeding Your Bees Feeding Your Bees

Feeding bees is a critical aspect of responsible beekeeping, ensuring the well-being of colonies during periods of nectar scarcity or in preparation for winter. Beekeepers often provide supplementary food, typically sugar syrup or fondant, to supplement natural forage.

Feeding is essential in early spring when bees' food reserves may be depleted and flowers are scarce. It's also crucial in late summer when bees prepare for winter by storing food. The feeding ratio typically varies, with stronger colonies needing less supplementation.

Proper feeding helps prevent starvation, maintains colony strength, and supports brood rearing, especially in times of dearth. Beekeepers must choose the right feeding method and maintain hygiene to prevent disease transmission.

However, overfeeding can disrupt the delicate balance within the hive, prompting swarming or reducing honey production. Beekeepers must strike a balance, ensuring that bees have access to natural forage while providing enough sustenance to foster colony health and productivity. Feeding is a dynamic aspect of beekeeping, adapting to seasonal and colony-specific needs, making it a vital skill for beekeepers to master.

Queen Management

Effective queen management is central to successful beekeeping. The queen is the heart of the colony, responsible for egg-laying and maintaining colony cohesion. Beekeepers must monitor queen health, ensuring she is productive and disease-free. If issues arise, requeening—introducing a new queen—is often necessary.

Queen management also involves controlling swarming behavior, a natural process where bees create a new queen and leave with a portion of the colony. Beekeepers can employ techniques like splitting colonies or removing queen cells to prevent swarms and maintain hive populations. Balancing a strong, productive queen with the overall colony's needs is a delicate task that influences honey production, hive stability, and genetic diversity. Queen management reflects a beekeeper's skill and commitment to sustaining healthy and thriving bee colonies.

Honey Extraction

Honey extraction is a crucial and rewarding step in beekeeping, allowing beekeepers to harvest the fruits of their colonies' labor. This process involves removing honey from the hive and preparing it for consumption or sale. Here are the key aspects of honey extraction:

- **Timing:** Harvesting honey should be done when the nectar flow is strong, typically in late spring or late summer, depending on the region. Beekeepers must consider the timing to maximize honey production while leaving sufficient stores for the colony.
- **Tools and Equipment:** Extracting honey requires specialized equipment, including honey extractors (centrifugal machines that spin honey out of frames), uncapping knives or forks, and filters to remove impurities.
- **Uncapping:** Before extracting, beekeepers must uncap the honeycomb frames to expose the honey. This can be done using hot knives or electric uncappers, ensuring minimal damage to the comb.
- **Extraction:** The frames are loaded into the honey extractor, which uses centrifugal force to release honey from the cells. The honey then collects at the bottom and can be drained into containers.
- **Filtering and Bottling:** The extracted honey is typically filtered to remove any remaining wax or debris. It is then poured into jars or containers for storage or sale.
- **Storing:** Proper storage of harvested honey is crucial to prevent crystallization and maintain its quality. Honey should be stored in a cool, dry place.
- **Safety and Hygiene:** Beekeepers must maintain high standards of cleanliness and hygiene throughout the extraction process to ensure the purity of the honey.
- **Respecting Bees:** While harvesting, beekeepers should prioritize minimizing disruption to the colony and avoiding damage to the comb.

Honey extraction is both an art and a science in beekeeping. It allows beekeepers to enjoy the sweet rewards of their efforts while ensuring the well-being and sustainability of their bee colonies.

Record Keeping

In beekeeping, meticulous record-keeping is akin to a hive's stored honey—both essential resources for success. Beekeepers maintain records to track hive health, behavior, and productivity. These records serve multiple purposes, shaping decisions and fostering responsible stewardship.

Health Monitoring:
Records document hive inspections, revealing patterns of disease, pests, and colony strength. Identifying issues early enables prompt intervention and treatment.

Hive History:
Keeping track of a hive's history, including queen introductions, splits, and requeening, helps manage genetics and predict colony behavior.

Forage and Seasons:
Recording forage availability and hive weight through seasons guides feeding and harvest timing, ensuring bees have ample sustenance.

Productivity:
Hive records detail honey and pollen collection, aiding in managing honey extraction and assessing the colony's efficiency.

Swarm Behavior:
Noting swarm preparations helps beekeepers take preventive measures, reducing colony loss.

Beekeeping Trends:
Records illuminate long-term trends, enabling beekeepers to adjust practices for sustainability and bee health.

Record keeping is not just an administrative task; it's a crucial tool that empowers beekeepers to make informed decisions, protect bee colonies, and cultivate thriving apiaries. It embodies the commitment to responsible and successful beekeeping practices.

Sustainable Beekeeping Practices

Sustainable beekeeping practices are the bedrock of responsible apiary management, reflecting a deep commitment to the well-being of honeybee colonies and the environment. They encompass a holistic approach to beekeeping that promotes harmony between bees and their ecosystem. Beekeepers embracing sustainability prioritize natural foraging, encouraging bees to rely on local, diverse sources of nectar and pollen rather than excessive supplemental feeding. They employ Integrated Pest Management (IPM) strategies, reducing chemical treatments, monitoring for pests and diseases, and opting for non-toxic alternatives when possible. Genetic diversity is fostered through thoughtful queen management to enhance colony resilience and adaptability.

Habitat preservation is a fundamental tenet, with beekeepers supporting pollinator-friendly landscapes, planting bee-friendly flora, and avoiding the use of harmful pesticides. Responsible honey harvesting practices prioritize minimal disruption to bees and leaving sufficient honey for overwintering.

Sustainable beekeeping practices not only benefit the bees and the beekeeper but also contribute to the broader preservation of these essential pollinators and their critical role in agriculture and biodiversity. Beekeepers who adopt these practices become stewards of both their own apiaries and the delicate balance of the natural world.

Chapter 6: Hive Inspections and Maintenance

Regular hive inspections are the backbone of effective beekeeping. In this chapter, we'll dive deep into the art and science of hive inspections, emphasizing their significance in understanding your colony, ensuring its health, and maximizing its productivity.

The Frequency of Inspections

Determining the right frequency for hive inspections is a delicate balance in beekeeping, akin to tuning an instrument to produce harmonious music. The timing of inspections can significantly impact colony health and productivity.
In the active season of spring and summer, bees are bustling with activity. Frequent inspections, typically every 7-10 days, are essential. These inspections enable beekeepers to monitor brood development, food stores, and the presence of the queen. It's a time when swarming tendencies must be closely watched, and hive management adjusted accordingly.

As the season transitions to fall and winter, bee activity slows. Inspections become less frequent, reducing to once a month or even less during the dormant winter months. These winter inspections are brief, focusing on assessing food stores and hive condensation levels, ensuring the colony has enough resources to survive.

The frequency of inspections varies with factors such as climate, hive size, and the beekeeper's objectives. It's a dynamic aspect of beekeeping, guided by the hive's needs and the beekeeper's experience. Over-inspecting can stress the colony, while infrequent inspections may miss critical issues. Thus, finding the right tempo of inspections is an art that beekeepers master as they become attuned to the rhythms of their hives, nurturing their colonies through the seasons with care and precision.

Tools and Equipment

Beekeeping is a craft that requires a specialized toolkit, akin to a surgeon's instruments or a chef's knives. These tools and equipment are not just accessories; they are extensions of the beekeeper's hands, essential for hive management and bee well-being.

1. **Hive Tool:**
The trusty hive tool is the beekeeper's Swiss Army knife. It's used for prying apart hive components, scraping off propolis or wax, and maneuvering frames during inspections.
2. **Smoker:**
The smoker emits cool smoke, a beekeeper's calming agent. It soothes bees, making inspections less stressful for both bees and beekeepers.
3. **Bee Suit and Veil:**
These protective garments shield beekeepers from stings. A good bee suit is breathable and comfortable, offering full-body protection.
4. **Gloves:**
Gloves provide hand protection while working with bees. Some beekeepers prefer lightweight gloves for dexterity, while others opt for heavier gloves for maximum protection.
5. **Bee Brush:**
A soft-bristle brush is used to gently remove bees from frames or comb during inspections.
6. **Frame Grip:**
Frame grips help beekeepers lift frames from the hive with ease, minimizing damage to bees and comb.
7. **Queen Marking Kit:**
This kit includes markers of different colors and a special cage for safely marking the queen for easy identification.
8. **Feeding Equipment:**
Feeders come in various types, like frame feeders, jar feeders, or entrance feeders, used to provide supplemental food to the colony when natural forage is scarce.
9. **Uncapping Tools:**

For honey extraction, uncapping knives or forks are used to remove the wax caps from honeycomb cells.

10. Extractor:
Extractors spin frames to extract honey. They come in manual and electric versions, allowing beekeepers to harvest honey efficiently.

Having the right tools and equipment ensures smooth hive inspections, honey harvesting, and overall hive management. Beekeepers meticulously maintain these instruments, treating them with care, as they are not just tools but the bridge that connects the beekeeper to their bees, fostering responsible stewardship and a thriving apiary.

Preparing for an Inspection

Before embarking on a hive inspection, a beekeeper engages in a pre-inspection ritual that is both methodical and respectful of the bees' domain. This preparation is like a conductor tuning an orchestra before a performance, setting the stage for a harmonious interaction between beekeeper and bees.

1. **Gather Equipment:**
   The beekeeper assembles the necessary tools: hive tool, smoker, protective gear, and any specific equipment for the inspection, such as a frame grip or queen marking kit.

2. **Choose the Right Time:**
   Selecting the right time for inspection is crucial. Bees are most active on warm, sunny days, so inspections are ideally conducted during these conditions.

3. **Light the Smoker:**
   The beekeeper lights the smoker and gives it time to produce cool, white smoke. This is the calming agent that will pacify the bees during the inspection.

4. **Don Protective Gear:**
   Beekeepers don their protective gear, ensuring it is in good condition and free from any openings that bees could exploit.

5. **Approach Calmly:**
   The beekeeper approaches the hive slowly and calmly, avoiding sudden movements or loud noises that might agitate the bees.

6. **Notify the Bees:**
   Some beekeepers tap the hive or gently blow a puff of smoke at the entrance to notify the bees of their presence, giving the colony a chance to adjust to the disturbance.

7. **Maintain Focus:**
   Throughout the inspection, the beekeeper maintains focus, moving with purpose and care. Frames are handled gently, and the hive is reassembled meticulously.

This preparatory phase not only ensures a safe and productive inspection but also demonstrates respect for the bees and their home. Beekeepers who approach inspections with patience and attention to detail not only gain valuable insights into their hives but also foster a harmonious relationship with their buzzing cohabitants.

The Hive Inspection Process

The hive inspection process is the heart of beekeeping, a choreographed exploration of the bee colony's inner workings. It begins with gently removing the hive's outer cover, followed by the inner cover, exposing the frames within. Each frame is lifted carefully, revealing the intricate world of bees. Beekeepers assess brood patterns, food stores, and the presence and health of the queen. During the inspection, bees are gently brushed aside, and the smoker is used to maintain calm. The inspection concludes with reassembling the hive with precision. This careful, methodical process not only ensures colony health but also fosters a bond between beekeeper and bees, a dance in which both partners thrive.

Recognizing and Addressing Issues

Beekeepers, as diligent stewards of their colonies, must be adept at recognizing and addressing issues that can afflict their bees. During hive inspections, keen observation is key. Signs of disease, like foulbrood or varroa mites, must be detected early to prevent outbreaks. Spotty brood patterns, a dwindling bee population, or the absence of a queen require swift action. If bees are running low on food stores, supplementary feeding is essential.
Addressing these issues may involve treatments, such as medication for disease or varroa control, requeening to ensure a productive colony, or adding food stores to prevent starvation. Effective issue recognition and timely interventions are critical for maintaining healthy, resilient colonies and ensuring the longevity of beekeeping endeavors.

Hive Hygiene

Hive hygiene is an essential aspect of beekeeping, mirroring the importance of cleanliness in human households. Inside the hive, bees meticulously maintain a pristine environment, removing debris, dead bees, and even diseased larvae. Beekeepers play a role in supporting this behavior by ensuring that hive components are free from contamination.

A clean hive is crucial for several reasons. It prevents the spread of disease and parasites, as well as reduces stress on the colony. Proper ventilation and spacing help prevent moisture buildup, which can lead to fungal growth. Adequate food stores are necessary, especially during winter months, to prevent starvation.

By prioritizing hive hygiene, beekeepers support the bees' natural behaviors and contribute to the overall health and productivity of their colonies.

Record Keeping and Documentation

Record keeping and documentation are the beekeeper's written narrative of their apiary's journey. These meticulous records capture essential details, including hive inspections, seasonal changes, and colony health. They serve as invaluable references, aiding in tracking hive performance, recognizing patterns, and making informed decisions.

Documentation includes hive notes, which detail colony behaviors, health assessments, and any issues observed. Seasonal records track honey production, forage availability, and bee population fluctuations. Queen records log her lineage and performance. Disease management notes document treatments and their outcomes.

Accurate records enable beekeepers to fine-tune their practices, adjust hive management, and plan strategically. They are not just data; they are the beekeeper's guidebook, fostering responsible stewardship, and ensuring the thriving of their bee colonies.

Beekeeping Ethics

Beekeeping ethics encapsulate the moral principles and responsibilities that guide the relationship between beekeepers and their bee colonies. Ethical beekeeping centers on the well-being of the bees, respecting their natural behaviors and needs.

It includes practices such as minimizing hive disruption during inspections, using non-toxic pest management methods, and ensuring bees have ample food and forage sources. Ethical beekeepers prioritize genetic diversity, avoiding practices that compromise colony health or long-term viability.

Responsible beekeeping recognizes that honeybees are not mere commodities but essential pollinators vital to ecosystems and agriculture. Beekeepers committed to ethical practices contribute to the sustainability of these remarkable insects and their invaluable role in maintaining biodiversity and food production.

Chapter 7: Collecting Honey and Hive Products

This section explores the culmination of a beekeeper's dedication - collecting honey and hive products. It's akin to agriculture's harvest season, where the rewards of meticulous beekeeping practices come to fruition.

Honey collection, a beekeeping highlight, symbolizes the fruits of labor. However, it's more than harvesting; it's a symphony of art and science. Beekeepers approach it with precision, care, and gratitude.

Beyond honey, hive products include beeswax, propolis, royal jelly, and pollen, each with unique properties. Their collection requires finesse and understanding.

This section unravels the intricacies of collecting these treasures. We explore honey extraction methods, from uncapping frames to spinning honey from combs. We delve into handling and processing beeswax, propolis, and other hive products.

The Honey Harvesting Process

Honey harvesting is a beekeeping crescendo, a harmonious collaboration between beekeeper and hive. It begins by gently uncapping the wax seals from honey-filled frames, revealing the liquid gold beneath. These frames are then placed in an extractor, where centrifugal force extracts honey without damaging the comb.

The liquid honey is collected, filtered, and stored in jars, ready to delight taste buds. However, honey harvesting is not just about procurement; it's a culmination of stewardship, respect, and gratitude for the bees' tireless work. It represents a shared journey with these remarkable insects, where the sweet reward is a testament to the enduring partnership between beekeeper and bees.

Harvesting Tools and Equipment

The honey harvesting process is a ballet that requires a specialized ensemble of tools and equipment. Key players include the uncapping knife, a heated tool that delicately removes the wax caps from honeycomb cells. The honey extractor takes center stage, spinning frames to release honey without damaging the comb.

Other essential tools include a strainer or filter to remove impurities, storage containers to preserve the liquid gold, and a settling tank to let air bubbles rise to the top. The ensemble also includes bee brushes, hive carriers, and bee suits to ensure a smooth and efficient harvest, safeguarding the bees' well-being while celebrating the sweet reward of their labor.

Extracting Honey

The process of extracting honey is the culmination of a beekeeper's careful stewardship and the tireless work of bees. It begins by removing the wax cappings from honey-filled frames, a meticulous task performed with an uncapping knife. These frames are then placed in a honey extractor, a spinning drum that uses centrifugal force to release honey from the comb without damaging it.

As the extractor whirls, honey flows from the frames and collects at the bottom. This liquid gold is then strained to remove any remaining wax particles or impurities. After this refining process, the honey is ready for storage in jars, preserving the pure, natural essence of the hive. Extracting honey is not just a mechanical process; it's a ritual of gratitude and celebration for the bountiful gift of nature and the enduring partnership between beekeeper and bees.

Processing Beeswax

Beeswax, a precious hive product, requires careful processing to unlock its versatility. After collecting wax cappings during honey extraction, beekeepers melt and filter the wax to remove impurities and any remaining honey residue.

Once purified, beeswax can take many forms. It's used to create beeswax candles, balms, cosmetics, and even beeswax wraps for eco-friendly food storage. In crafting, it serves as a natural, aromatic ingredient. The beeswax processing journey is a testament to the beekeeper's resourcefulness, making the most of every gift the hive provides and ensuring nothing goes to waste. It's a continuation of the partnership with the bees, turning their labor into products that benefit both beekeeper and the environment.

Harvesting Propolis

Propolis, the hive's natural adhesive and protective resin, is a valuable hive product with diverse applications. Beekeepers harvest it by scraping it from hive components like frames and inner covers.

Once collected, propolis is cleaned and prepared for use. Its medicinal and therapeutic properties make it a sought-after ingredient in natural remedies, such as tinctures, salves, and throat sprays. Propolis also has applications in cosmetics and even musical instrument varnishes due to its unique qualities.

Harvesting propolis is a sustainable practice that optimizes hive resources while offering beekeepers a valuable byproduct. It's a testament to the beekeeper's ingenuity and resourcefulness in harnessing every aspect of the hive's bounty.

Royal Jelly Extraction

Royal jelly, the nutrient-rich secretion produced by worker bees, is a prized hive product. Extracting royal jelly is a precise and delicate process. Beekeepers employ specialized tools to carefully remove royal jelly from individual cells within the hive.

Once collected, royal jelly must be handled with care and refrigerated to maintain its freshness and nutritional value. It has a variety of applications, particularly in dietary supplements and cosmetics due to its potential health benefits for humans.

The extraction of royal jelly exemplifies the beekeeper's commitment to both the bees and the hive's valuable resources. It showcases the delicate balance between responsible stewardship and the exploration of nature's treasures within the hive.

Beehive Products Management

Efficient hive product management is an integral part of responsible beekeeping. Beekeepers must navigate the delicate balance between harvesting hive products and ensuring the hive's well-being. This process involves timing honey extraction to coincide with surplus production, leaving enough for the bees during winter.

Proper storage of harvested products, such as honey and beeswax, is essential to maintain their quality. Containers must be airtight to prevent crystallization of honey and protect beeswax from contamination.

Effective hive product management underscores the beekeeper's commitment to sustainability, respecting the bees' hard work and preserving the hive's integrity. It's a testament to the beekeeper's role as a conscientious steward of the bees and their valuable contributions to both the hive and human livelihoods.

Ethical Harvesting

Ethical harvesting in beekeeping is a reflection of responsible stewardship and respect for the hive's inhabitants. It emphasizes the well-being of the bees, ensuring that their needs are met before any surplus is collected. This principle involves taking only what the colony can spare without compromising its health or ability to survive.

Ethical harvesting also extends to humane practices, such as minimizing bee stress during the process and avoiding harm to the queen or brood. It includes the use of non-toxic methods in hive product collection and a commitment to sustainable practices that preserve both bee populations and their habitats.

Beekeepers who prioritize ethical harvesting demonstrate a profound connection to the natural world, acknowledging the bees as partners rather than mere resources. Their approach not only fosters thriving colonies but also promotes responsible beekeeping practices that benefit both bees and the broader environment.

Chapter 8: Dealing with Common Beekeeping Challenges

Beekeeping, like any agricultural pursuit, comes with its share of challenges and obstacles. In this chapter, we'll explore the common issues that beekeepers often encounter and provide practical solutions to address these challenges effectively.

Pests and Parasites

Pests and parasites pose significant challenges to bee colonies, and beekeepers play a crucial role in managing these threats. Varroa mites, small hive beetles, and wax moths are among the most notorious invaders. These intruders can weaken, disrupt, or even devastate colonies if left unchecked.

Beekeepers employ integrated pest management (IPM) strategies, which include monitoring, chemical treatments as a last resort, and fostering strong, healthy colonies that are more resilient to infestations. Maintaining good hive hygiene, using screened bottom boards, and providing access to natural forage all contribute to reducing the risk of pests and parasites.

Effectively managing pests and parasites is a testament to the beekeeper's dedication to colony health and the crucial role they play in preserving bee populations in the face of these challenges.

Diseases

Bee colonies are susceptible to various diseases, posing significant threats to their survival. Nosema, foulbrood, and chalkbrood are some common maladies that can weaken and decimate bee populations.

Beekeepers must be vigilant in disease detection and management. Regular hive inspections, diagnostic tests, and quarantine measures are essential to prevent disease spread. Treatment options may include antibiotics or organic remedies, depending on the disease and beekeeper's preference.

Effective disease management is not only about protecting individual colonies but also safeguarding entire bee populations. Beekeepers who prioritize disease prevention and control contribute to the overall health and resilience of honeybee populations, ensuring their continued role as vital pollinators in ecosystems and agriculture.

Robbing and Predation

In the world of bees, competition for resources is fierce, and colonies are not exempt from threats. Robbing, when one colony pillages the honey stores of another, can lead to the downfall of weaker hives. Beekeepers must remain vigilant to spot signs of robbing, such as heightened aggression and fighting at the hive entrance.

Predation from other insects, birds, or mammals also poses risks. Skunks, bears, and certain bird species are known culprits. Beekeepers employ protective measures, like electric fencing or guard dogs, to deter predators.

Managing robbing and predation is essential for hive survival. Beekeepers play a critical role in defending their colonies, ensuring the well-being of their bees, and preserving the hive's resources.

Swarming

Swarming is a natural and fascinating aspect of bee behavior, but it can pose challenges for beekeepers. Recognizing the signs of an impending swarm is crucial. These signs may include a crowded hive, the presence of queen cells, and increased drone activity.

Preventing swarming involves maintaining ample space within the hive, ensuring the queen is healthy and young, and managing colony growth through techniques like splitting or providing additional supers.

However, if a colony does swarm, beekeepers must act swiftly to capture and rehive the swarm, preserving valuable genetic material and preventing the loss of a portion of the bee population. Understanding swarming dynamics and strategies is essential for beekeepers to manage and harness this natural process to their advantage.

Queen Issues

The queen bee is the heart of the hive, responsible for laying eggs and maintaining colony cohesion. Queen issues can significantly impact a colony's stability. Beekeepers must monitor for problems like a failing or absent queen, supersedure, or swarming tendencies.

If the queen fails to perform adequately or is absent, the hive's population dwindles, and its productivity declines. Supersedure, where the colony replaces the queen, may occur for various reasons, including age or health issues.

Beekeepers address queen issues by requeening, introducing a new, vigorous queen to revitalize the hive. Identifying and resolving queen problems promptly is crucial to maintain a healthy, thriving colony and ensure the continued success of the beekeeping endeavor.

Environmental Factors

Beekeeping success is intricately linked to environmental conditions. Temperature, rainfall, forage availability, and local flora all influence hive health and productivity. Beekeepers must adapt their practices to regional climate and seasons, as bees' foraging behavior, reproduction, and food stores are profoundly affected.

Environmental factors also include exposure to pesticides and pollutants, which can harm bees and their colonies. Sustainable practices, such as planting pollinator-friendly flora and avoiding harmful chemicals, help mitigate these threats.

Beekeepers who understand and work in harmony with their local environment are better equipped to support strong, resilient colonies. Environmental consciousness and adaptation are essential facets of responsible beekeeping and the preservation of these invaluable pollinators.

Seasonal Management

Beekeeping is a dynamic practice, shaped by the changing seasons. Each season brings distinct challenges and opportunities for beekeepers.

- **Spring**: This season marks the renewal of bee activity. Beekeepers monitor colony strength and health, encourage brood rearing, and assess food stores.
- **Summer**: Bees are at the height of their foraging activity, collecting nectar and pollen. Beekeepers focus on honey extraction and swarm prevention.
- **Fall**: As forage wanes, beekeepers ensure colonies have adequate winter stores. They may also treat for pests and diseases.
- **Winter**: Bees cluster to conserve warmth. Beekeepers provide insulation, ventilation, and emergency feeding if necessary.

Adapting to seasonal changes is vital for colony survival and productivity. Beekeepers who synchronize their management practices with nature's rhythm optimize their beekeeping endeavors.

Chapter 9: Beekeeping Seasons and Annual Hive Care

Successful beekeeping requires a deep understanding of the changing seasons and the specific needs of your bee colony throughout the year. In this chapter, we will explore the four seasons and the corresponding tasks and considerations for each season in beekeeping.

Spring: The Season of Renewal

Spring is a time of renewal and growth for bee colonies. During this season, we'll cover:

- **Spring Hive Inspections**: Inspect the hive to assess colony strength, queen health, and food stores.
- **Swarm Prevention**: Implement swarm prevention techniques to maintain a strong colony.
- **Supplemental Feeding**: If necessary, provide sugar syrup to support colony growth until nectar flow is abundant.

Summer: The Season of Abundance

Summer brings abundant forage opportunities for bees. In this season:

- **Honey Production**: Monitor honey supers and extract surplus honey when appropriate.
- **Queen Health**: Ensure the queen is laying eggs consistently to maintain a robust population.
- **Hive Ventilation**: Manage hive ventilation to prevent overheating during hot weather.

Fall: The Season of Preparation

Fall is a crucial time for bees to prepare for the upcoming winter. Tasks include:

- **Hive Inspection**: Assess the hive's food stores, population, and overall health.
- **Varroa Mite Management**: Implement mite control measures to ensure colony survival.
- **Feeding and Winterization**: Provide supplementary feeding and insulate the hive for winter.

Winter: The Season of Rest

Winter is a challenging time for beekeepers and their colonies. During winter:

- **Monitoring**: Check on the hive periodically to ensure the bees have enough food.
- **Winter Feeding**: Supplemental feeding may be necessary if honey stores are low.
- **Protecting from Cold**: Insulate and protect the hive from extreme cold, wind, and moisture.

Annual Hive Care

In addition to season-specific tasks, there are annual hive care practices that should be part of your beekeeping routine, regardless of the season. These include:

- **Equipment Maintenance**: Clean and maintain your beekeeping equipment, including hive components and tools.
- **Hive Rotation**: Rotate frames and comb to promote hive hygiene and prevent diseases.
- **Record Review**: Review your hive inspection records and assess the overall health and performance of your colonies.

Understanding the unique requirements of each season and performing the appropriate tasks is vital for the well-being and productivity of your bee colony. By aligning your beekeeping practices with the changing seasons, you'll foster strong, resilient colonies that can thrive year after year.

Chapter 10: Expanding Your Beekeeping Operation

As you gain experience and confidence in beekeeping, you may find yourself eager to expand your operation. This chapter explores various ways to expand your beekeeping endeavors, whether as a hobbyist or a budding beekeeping entrepreneur.

Increasing Hive Count

One of the most straightforward ways to expand your beekeeping operation is by increasing the number of hives in your apiary. We'll discuss methods for starting new colonies, including splitting existing hives, buying nucleus colonies, or capturing swarms.

Producing Nucleus Colonies

Nucleus colonies, or nucs, are smaller bee colonies that can be used for various purposes, such as selling, replacing queens, or starting new hives. We'll explore the process of creating nucs and their benefits in beekeeping expansion.

Queen Rearing and Breeding

Becoming proficient in queen rearing and breeding allows you to have more control over your bee genetics and colony dynamics. We'll introduce you to the principles of queen rearing and the steps involved in selecting, raising, and introducing new queens.

Honey and Hive Product Sales

If you have surplus honey, beeswax, or other hive products, you can consider selling them. We'll provide guidance on selling honey and hive products, including legal considerations, packaging, and marketing strategies.

Pollination Services

Offering your hives for pollination services can be a lucrative venture, especially if you have access to agricultural areas that require pollinators. We'll discuss how to enter the pollination market and what to consider when offering your bees for pollination contracts.

Beekeeping Education

Sharing your knowledge and expertise can be a rewarding way to expand your beekeeping operation. We'll explore options for offering beekeeping courses, workshops, or consulting services to others interested in beekeeping.

Diversifying Hive Products

Beyond honey, beeswax, and propolis, there are numerous hive products you can explore, such as royal jelly, pollen, and bee venom. We'll introduce you to these lesser-known products and how to harvest and market them.

Sustainable Practices in Expansion

As you expand your beekeeping operation, it's essential to maintain sustainable practices to ensure the health of your bees and the environment. We'll revisit sustainable beekeeping principles and how they apply to expansion efforts.

Expanding your beekeeping operation can bring new challenges and opportunities. Whether your goal is to increase honey production, share your knowledge, or offer pollination services, careful planning and dedication to responsible beekeeping practices will help you succeed in your expansion endeavors.

Chapter II: Bee Health and Disease Management

Maintaining the health of your bee colony is paramount to successful beekeeping. In this chapter, we will delve into bee health and disease management, equipping you with the knowledge and strategies to keep your bees thriving.

Monitoring Bee Health

Regular hive inspections are your first line of defense in monitoring bee health. We'll revisit the importance of thorough inspections and discuss what to look for when assessing the health of your colony.

Common Bee Diseases

Beekeeping, like any agricultural endeavor, faces the challenge of disease management. Healthy colonies are essential for productive hives and pollination services, making it imperative for beekeepers to understand and address common bee diseases. In this comprehensive exploration, we delve into five significant bee diseases, discussing their symptoms, causes, prevention, and management strategies.

1. **American Foulbrood (AFB)**

Symptoms: AFB is a highly contagious bacterial disease primarily affecting honeybee larvae. Infected larvae exhibit a brown, sunken appearance with spotty scales on their bodies.

Causes: AFB is caused by the bacterium Paenibacillus larvae. It spreads through spore transmission and is highly resilient, surviving in hives for extended periods.

Management: The management of AFB requires vigilance and strict adherence to prevention measures. Infected hives must be destroyed, and beekeepers must employ sanitation practices, including regular comb replacement and proper hive hygiene.

2. European Foulbrood (EFB)
Symptoms: EFB primarily affects larvae, causing them to turn yellow, die, and decompose. Unlike AFB, EFB-infected larvae don't exhibit a ropiness or foul odor.

Causes: EFB is caused by the bacterium Melissococcus plutonius. It spreads through spore transmission but is generally less destructive than AFB.

Management: Management involves improving hive conditions to boost colony health and resistance to EFB. Antibiotics may be administered in severe cases, and hive inspections should be regular to detect and isolate affected colonies.

2. **Chalkbrood**

Symptoms: Chalkbrood, a fungal disease, causes infected larvae to become hard and chalk-like in appearance. They resemble small, white mummies.

Causes: Chalkbrood is caused by the fungus Ascosphaera apis. It often occurs during damp or cool conditions.

Management: While chalkbrood is less destructive than bacterial diseases, management includes improving hive ventilation and reducing moisture levels. Infected frames should be removed, and beekeepers may employ practices to encourage colony hygiene.

3. **Nosema**

Symptoms: Nosema is a gut parasite that affects adult bees, leading to reduced colony strength and productivity. Infected bees may exhibit dysentery, with fecal matter near hive entrances.

Causes: Nosema is caused by microsporidian parasites, primarily Nosema apis and Nosema ceranae.

Management: Managing Nosema includes maintaining good hive hygiene, providing clean water sources, and avoiding stressors. Some treatments, like fumagillin, can be used to mitigate Nosema infections.

4. **Sacbrood Virus**

Symptoms: Sacbrood virus affects bee larvae, causing them to develop sac-like, fluid-filled bodies and eventually die. Infected larvae resemble tiny, opaque sacs.

Causes: Sacbrood virus is a viral infection that can spread within a hive.

Management: Sacbrood virus management involves maintaining a strong and healthy colony. While there is no direct treatment for the virus, keeping hives robust and stress-free can reduce its impact.

Prevention and Biosecurity

Preventing these diseases is key to hive health. Beekeepers should follow biosecurity measures such as cleaning equipment, practicing good hygiene, and monitoring hives regularly for signs of disease. Additionally, selecting disease-resistant bee strains and providing proper nutrition can bolster colony immunity.

Varroa Mites

Varroa destructor, commonly known as Varroa mites, stands as one of the most significant threats to bee colonies worldwide. These tiny parasitic mites attach to adult bees and, more destructively, to developing bee larvae, feeding on their hemolymph (bee "blood") and transmitting viruses.
Varroa mites weaken bees, causing deformities, reducing lifespan, and stunting colony growth. Left unmanaged, they can devastate entire hives. Beekeepers employ various strategies to control Varroa mite infestations, including chemical treatments, organic methods, and the promotion of hygienic bee behavior.
Managing Varroa mites is an ongoing battle in beekeeping, underscoring the need for vigilance and adaptive practices to safeguard honeybee populations and ensure their vital role in pollination and agriculture.

Small Hive Beetles and Wax Moths

We'll also explore the management of small hive beetles and wax moths, two common hive pests that can weaken colonies if left unchecked. You'll learn how to recognize their presence and take appropriate measures.

Integrated Pest Management (IPM)

Integrated Pest Management (IPM) is a comprehensive strategy that beekeepers employ to address various pests and diseases, with a primary focus on sustainability and minimizing chemical intervention. IPM integrates multiple practices to effectively manage issues like Varroa mites, keeping hive health and productivity at the forefront.

Key components of IPM in beekeeping include:

1. Monitoring: Regular hive inspections and assessments are crucial to identify pest and disease levels accurately. Monitoring helps beekeepers make informed decisions about the timing and necessity of interventions.

2. Cultural Practices: Beekeepers can implement cultural practices such as brood break management or drone trapping to disrupt pests' life cycles.

3. Mechanical Control: Techniques like screened bottom boards, which can hinder Varroa mite reproduction, are part of IPM.

4. Biological Control: Some beneficial organisms, like predatory mites, can naturally control pest populations.

5. Chemical Control (as a last resort): Chemical treatments are used sparingly and strategically when other methods prove insufficient.

IPM promotes resilience within bee colonies while minimizing chemical exposure and its potential impact on hive health. It reflects beekeepers' commitment to responsible stewardship, preserving both pollinators and the ecosystems they serve.

Treatment-Free Beekeeping

Treatment-free beekeeping is an approach that emphasizes minimal intervention and the reliance on natural bee behaviors and adaptations to manage pests and diseases. It stands in contrast to conventional beekeeping, which often employs chemical treatments to combat issues like Varroa mites and diseases.

In treatment-free beekeeping, the emphasis is on fostering genetically robust bee populations that can withstand pest and disease pressures. This approach involves:

1. **Selective Breeding:** Beekeepers select and propagate colonies with resistance traits, promoting genetic diversity and resilience.

2. **Small Cell Beekeeping:** Some practitioners advocate for smaller cell sizes in comb foundation, arguing that it may help mitigate Varroa mite infestations.

3. **Integrated Pest Management (IPM):** While treatment-free beekeepers avoid synthetic chemicals, they may still utilize IPM techniques, such as drone trapping or brood breaks, to disrupt pest life cycles.

Treatment-free beekeeping reflects a commitment to sustainable, naturalistic practices that align with the well-being of both bees and the environment. However, it requires careful management, observation, and a willingness to accept some colony losses as part of the broader philosophy of beekeeping in harmony with nature.

Biosecurity and Preventive Measures

Preventing the introduction and spread of diseases and pests is essential. We'll discuss biosecurity measures, hive sanitation, and quarantine procedures to protect your bees from external threats.

Chapter 12: Beekeeping and Environmental Conservation

Beekeeping and environmental conservation go hand in hand. In this chapter, we'll explore the critical role that beekeepers can play in preserving natural ecosystems and supporting the well-being of pollinators.

The Importance of Bees in Ecosystems

Bees, as pollinators, play a vital role in ecosystems. We'll delve into the significance of bees in pollinating plants, including agricultural crops and wildflowers, and how their activities contribute to biodiversity.

Pesticide Awareness

Pesticides can harm bees and other pollinators. We'll discuss the potential risks of pesticides and the importance of using them responsibly. You'll learn about alternative pest management strategies that are less harmful to bees.

Forage and Habitat Enhancement

Supporting bee health and conservation involves providing bees with ample forage and suitable habitats. We'll explore ways to enhance forage availability through planting pollinator-friendly plants and creating bee-friendly gardens.

Avoiding Invasive Plants

Some invasive plant species can outcompete native plants and disrupt local ecosystems. We'll discuss the importance of avoiding invasive plants in your beekeeping endeavors and selecting regionally appropriate vegetation.

Reducing Environmental Footprint

Sustainable beekeeping practices can minimize your environmental footprint. We'll revisit sustainable beekeeping principles, including reduced chemical use, hive hygiene, and ethical harvesting, and how they contribute to environmental conservation.

Participating in Citizen Science

Engaging in citizen science projects can help you contribute valuable data to research efforts focused on bee health and habitat conservation. We'll introduce you to citizen science initiatives and how you can get involved.

Promoting Pollinator-Friendly Policies

Advocacy and community engagement can play a role in promoting policies that protect pollinators and their habitats. We'll discuss ways to engage with local and national organizations to advocate for pollinator-friendly policies.

Educating Others

Educating your community about the importance of pollinators and bee conservation is a powerful way to raise awareness. We'll provide tips and resources for effectively communicating the value of bees to others.

Supporting Native Bees

Native bees also play a crucial role in pollination. We'll touch on ways to support and conserve native bee species alongside honeybees.

Chapter 13: Beekeeping Challenges and Adaptation

Beekeeping is a dynamic endeavor that often requires adaptation to changing circumstances. In this chapter, we'll explore the challenges that beekeepers may face and strategies to adapt and thrive in the ever-evolving world of beekeeping.

Climate Change

Climate change can impact beekeeping in various ways, from altered flowering seasons to increased environmental stressors. We'll discuss the effects of climate change on bees and how beekeepers can adapt their practices to mitigate these challenges.

Habitat Loss

As natural habitats diminish, bees face a loss of forage and nesting sites. We'll explore how habitat loss affects bees and ways beekeepers can contribute to habitat restoration and preservation.

Pesticide Exposure

Pesticide exposure remains a significant concern for bees. We'll revisit the importance of pesticide awareness and discuss strategies for minimizing pesticide exposure for your colonies.

Bee Health Issues

New bee health challenges can emerge, requiring beekeepers to stay informed and adapt. We'll provide guidance on staying up-to-date with the latest research and adapting your management practices accordingly.

Market Changes

The beekeeping industry and honey market can experience fluctuations. We'll discuss how beekeepers can adapt to market changes and explore alternative revenue streams, such as value-added hive products or pollination services.

Regulatory Changes

Beekeeping regulations and guidelines may change over time. We'll emphasize the importance of staying compliant with local regulations and adapting to any new requirements.

Technology and Innovation

he world of beekeeping is experiencing a technological revolution. As beekeepers grapple with the challenges of maintaining healthy colonies and preserving pollinators in an ever-changing environment, advancements in technology are offering unprecedented opportunities to enhance hive management, mitigate threats, and safeguard honeybee populations.

1. **Hive Monitoring Systems:**

Hive monitoring systems are at the forefront of beekeeping technology. These systems typically incorporate sensors, cameras, and communication devices to provide real-time data about hive conditions. Here's how they're making a difference:

- **Temperature and Humidity Sensors:** These sensors help beekeepers monitor hive climate, critical for brood development and overall colony health. Abnormalities in temperature or humidity can signal potential issues, allowing beekeepers to take timely action.
- **Weight Sensors:** Weight sensors provide valuable insights into honey stores and nectar flow. Beekeepers can determine when to add or remove supers, preventing swarming and ensuring bees have sufficient food.

- **Camera Systems:** Hive cameras offer a peek inside the hive without disturbing the bees. Beekeepers can visually inspect frames for brood patterns, honey reserves, and signs of disease.

- **Remote Monitoring:** Many systems allow beekeepers to access hive data remotely through smartphone apps or web interfaces, reducing the need for physical hive inspections and minimizing bee disturbance.

- **Data Analytics:** The data collected by monitoring systems can be analyzed to identify trends, patterns, and anomalies. This information helps beekeepers make informed decisions about hive management.

2. **Precision Beekeeping:**

Precision beekeeping is akin to precision agriculture, utilizing technology to optimize beekeeping practices. Some aspects include:

- **GPS Tracking:** Beekeepers can attach GPS trackers to hive components or individual bees to monitor foraging patterns and assess the impact of land use changes on bee forage.

- **Phenology Models:** Data-driven models can predict when plants will bloom and nectar flows will occur, helping beekeepers plan hive interventions and migrations more effectively.

- **Robotic Hive Management:** Research is ongoing into robotic systems that can assist with hive inspections, frame extraction, and even disease detection, reducing the physical demands on beekeepers.

3. **Disease Detection and Management:**

Technology is aiding in early disease detection and management, crucial for hive health. Some innovations include:

- **Smart Hive Components:** Frames with embedded sensors can monitor bee activity, sound patterns, and hygiene behaviors, alerting beekeepers to potential disease outbreaks.

- **Machine Learning and AI:** AI algorithms can analyze images of frames, brood, and bees to identify disease symptoms, such as foulbrood or Varroa mite infestations.

- **Biotechnology:** Researchers are exploring biotechnology solutions, such as RNA interference (RNAi), to target specific bee pathogens and pests.

4. **Genetic Analysis:**

Genetic analysis is helping beekeepers breed more resilient and disease-resistant bee strains. Techniques like DNA sequencing and marker-assisted selection can identify desirable traits and inform selective breeding programs.

5. **Pollinator-Friendly Apps and Tools:**

There's a growing array of apps and online tools designed to support pollinator-friendly landscaping and planting. These resources help individuals and communities create bee-friendly habitats by selecting native plants, reducing pesticide use, and providing nesting sites.

6. Education and Outreach:
Online platforms and social media are powerful tools for beekeeping education and outreach. Beekeepers can share experiences, exchange knowledge, and mobilize efforts to protect bees and their habitats.

7. Citizen Science:
Citizen science initiatives leverage technology to engage beekeepers and the general public in data collection. Projects like the Great Sunflower Project and the Bee Informed Partnership rely on volunteers to monitor and report bee activity and health, contributing to broader research efforts.

The Benefits of Embracing Technology:

Embracing technology and innovation in beekeeping offers several potential benefits:

- **Improved Hive Health:** Real-time monitoring allows for early intervention in cases of disease, pest infestations, or resource shortages, ultimately leading to healthier colonies.
- **Efficiency:** Technology streamlines hive management tasks, reducing labor and time requirements for beekeepers.
- **Data-Driven Decision-Making:** Analyzing hive data enables evidence-based decisions, optimizing beekeeping practices, and increasing colony productivity.
- **Education and Collaboration:** Online platforms facilitate knowledge sharing, collaboration, and the dissemination of best practices among beekeepers and researchers.
- **Research Advancements:** Technology accelerates research into bee biology, behavior, and health, leading to breakthroughs in disease management and breeding programs.
- **Environmental Stewardship:** Precision beekeeping and pollinator-friendly tools contribute to the preservation of bee habitats and the promotion of responsible land management.

Challenges and Considerations:

While beekeeping technology offers tremendous potential, it also presents challenges and considerations:

- **Cost:** Some technology solutions can be expensive, potentially limiting access for smaller-scale beekeepers.
- **Data Security:** Protecting hive data from cybersecurity threats is critical to prevent unauthorized access and data breaches.
- **Dependency:** Overreliance on technology may reduce hands-on beekeeping skills and experience.
- **Ethical Concerns:** Some beekeepers may have ethical concerns about the use of certain technologies, such as genetic modification.

In conclusion, technology and innovation are reshaping the landscape of beekeeping. From hive monitoring systems to genetic analysis and precision beekeeping, these advancements are empowering beekeepers to overcome challenges, protect honeybee populations, and contribute to the vital role of bees in pollination and agriculture. Balancing the benefits of technology with ethical, environmental, and cost considerations is essential as beekeeping continues to evolve in the 21st century.

Community and Collaboration

Building a network of fellow beekeepers and collaborating with experts can be valuable for problem-solving and adaptation. We'll discuss the benefits of joining beekeeping associations and participating in knowledge-sharing communities.

Resilience and Flexibility Adaptability is a key trait for successful beekeepers. We'll emphasize the importance of resilience and flexibility in the face of challenges, enabling you to adjust your beekeeping practices as needed.

Chapter 14: Beekeeping and the Future

In this final chapter, we will peer into the future of beekeeping and explore the possibilities, innovations, and trends that may shape the world of beekeeping in the years to come.

Technological Advancements

The integration of technology into beekeeping continues to evolve. We'll discuss the potential impact of advancements such as remote hive monitoring, precision beekeeping, and data-driven management on the industry.

Sustainable Practices Sustainability is a growing concern, and beekeepers are increasingly adopting eco-friendly practices. We'll explore how sustainable beekeeping methods, from chemical reduction to habitat restoration, will become even more central to the future of beekeeping.

Urban Beekeeping

In recent years, urban beekeeping has emerged as a flourishing trend, fostering a harmonious coexistence between bees and city dwellers. This practice involves keeping beehives within urban and suburban environments, offering unique benefits and confronting distinctive challenges.

Benefits of Urban Beekeeping:

1. **Pollinator Support:** Urban areas, despite their concrete expanses, often contain pockets of greenery in the form of parks, gardens, and flowering trees. Urban bees can forage on these diverse floral resources, contributing to local pollination efforts. In some cases, urban beekeeping can bolster the pollination of nearby community gardens and urban farms, enhancing food production.

2. **Environmental Awareness:** Urban beekeeping provides an opportunity for city residents to connect with nature and gain a deeper understanding of the critical role bees play in ecosystems. Educating urban populations about bee conservation and biodiversity can lead to more environmentally conscious practices.

3. **Local Honey Production:** Urban beekeepers can harvest honey that reflects the unique flavors of the city's floral diversity. This local honey can be prized for its distinct taste and potential health benefits due to its pollen content.

4. **Community Engagement:** Beekeeping can foster a sense of community and collaboration. Urban beekeeping clubs, workshops, and educational events bring people together to learn about bee biology, hive management, and sustainable practices.

Challenges of Urban Beekeeping:

1. **Limited Forage:** While cities offer floral resources, the diversity and abundance of forage can be limited compared to rural areas. Urban beekeepers must carefully select hive locations near suitable forage to ensure their colonies thrive.

2. **Pesticide Exposure:** Urban environments may expose bees to pesticides from ornamental plants, lawns, and nearby agricultural areas. Managing pesticide exposure is a significant challenge for urban beekeepers.

3. **Space Constraints:** Urban settings often impose space constraints, requiring creative hive placement solutions. Bees must coexist with human activities, necessitating careful hive placement and management to prevent conflicts.

4. **Regulations:** Urban beekeepers may encounter local regulations and zoning laws that govern hive placement, hive density, and safety. Navigating these regulations can be complex and varies by location.

5. **Bee Health:** Urban colonies may face increased stressors, such as air pollution, heat islands, and limited forage, which can impact bee health and vitality.

Pollinator Health Initiatives

Efforts to protect pollinators and their habitats are gaining momentum. We'll examine how beekeepers can contribute to and benefit from pollinator health initiatives and collaborations with conservation organizations.

Bee-Friendly Agriculture

Farmers and beekeepers are increasingly working together to create bee-friendly agricultural landscapes. We'll explore the potential for partnerships that support both agriculture and bee health.

Research and Education

The importance of research and education in beekeeping cannot be overstated. We'll discuss the role of ongoing research in advancing beekeeping practices and the importance of educating the next generation of beekeepers.

Market Trends

The honey and hive product market is evolving, with consumers seeking local, sustainable, and high-quality products. We'll examine emerging market trends and how beekeepers can capitalize on them.

Environmental Conservation

Environmental conservation will continue to be a critical focus. We'll look at the ways beekeepers can contribute to preserving natural ecosystems and the health of pollinators.

Global Collaboration

Beekeeping is a global endeavor, and collaboration among beekeepers worldwide is increasingly essential. We'll explore the potential for global partnerships and knowledge sharing to address common challenges.

Chapter 15: Your Beekeeping Legacy

In the closing chapter of your beekeeping journey, we turn our gaze towards the legacy you can leave behind as a dedicated beekeeper. Beyond the sweet honey, beeswax, and the satisfaction of nurturing thriving hives, your legacy in beekeeping carries a profound impact on your community, the wider world of beekeeping, and the future of pollinators.

Beekeeping as a Lifelong Journey

Beekeeping is not merely a hobby; it's a lifelong journey, an odyssey of discovery, wonder, and growth. Your initiation into beekeeping marked the beginning of a captivating adventure, one that offered not just the golden liquid of honey but also a taste of personal growth, satisfaction, and boundless joy.
Every beekeeping season brought with it lessons in patience, resilience, and attentiveness. You learned to read the hive's subtle cues, deciphering the ever-shifting moods of your colonies. Through successes and challenges, your beekeeping journey was an inexhaustible source of personal enrichment, fostering a profound connection to the natural world.

Passing on Knowledge

As you reflect on your beekeeping odyssey, consider the wisdom and experience you've amassed over the years. Sharing your knowledge with the beekeeping community is an invaluable contribution to beekeeping's legacy. Becoming a mentor or educator to future beekeepers is a way to ensure that the collective wisdom of beekeeping continues to flourish.
Mentoring is a beacon of guidance for novices, offering them a hand to hold as they navigate the intricate world of beekeeping. By passing on your knowledge, you enable others to embark on their own beekeeping journeys, instilling in them a reverence for these remarkable creatures and a commitment to their care.

Promoting Bee Health

The health of your bee colonies is a testament to your stewardship. Healthy and thriving hives contribute not only to your personal satisfaction but also to broader bee conservation efforts. By maintaining disease-free colonies and fostering robust, flourishing hives, you participate in preserving bee populations and promoting their well-being.

Healthy hives ensure the vitality of honeybee populations, which in turn safeguards the pollination of countless plants and the sustenance of ecosystems. Your commitment to bee health is an integral part of your beekeeping legacy, a gift to both the bees and the world they pollinate.

Supporting Local Pollinators

Beekeepers are not just stewards of honeybees; they have the power to make a difference in their local ecosystems. Beyond the garden walls, beekeepers play a pivotal role in supporting native pollinators and maintaining the delicate ecological balance.
The habitats you create, the wildflowers you plant, and the conscientious land management you practice all contribute to a harmonious coexistence with nature. By nurturing not only honeybees but also native pollinators, you ensure that the web of life remains intact, benefiting not just your bee colonies but the broader environment.

Advocacy and Conservation

Advocacy for bee health and conservation is an essential facet of your beekeeping legacy. As a beekeeper, you have a unique vantage point from which to observe the challenges and threats facing pollinators. Your voice carries weight in local and global discussions on pollinator protection and conservation.
Engaging in advocacy efforts allows you to be a beacon of change. You can collaborate with like-minded individuals and organizations, championing bee-friendly policies, raising awareness about pesticide use, and participating in habitat restoration projects. Your advocacy efforts ripple through the beekeeping community, inspiring collective action in safeguarding pollinators for future generations.

Community Building

Beekeeping transcends the solitary act of hive inspection. It can be a source of community and connection, fostering relationships and collaboration among beekeepers and enthusiasts. The shared passion for bees brings people together, creating a tapestry of camaraderie and support. Through beekeeping clubs, workshops, and community events, you can be an architect of unity within the beekeeping world. Building a strong, interconnected community ensures that beekeepers continue to learn from one another, share experiences, and collectively address the challenges facing bees.

Sustainable Practices

Sustainable beekeeping practices are the cornerstone of your beekeeping legacy. As stewards of the land, you understand the delicate interplay between bees and the environment. Leaving a positive environmental impact means practicing sustainable beekeeping and passing down these practices to future generations.

Sustainability involves responsible hive management, natural forage promotion, and conscientious hive placement. It entails a commitment to reducing environmental stressors, including pesticide exposure and habitat loss. By prioritizing sustainability, you leave a lasting mark on beekeeping and contribute to a future where bees thrive alongside human activity.

Inspiring Others

Your beekeeping journey has the power to inspire others. Your dedication to bee stewardship, advocacy, and conservation can serve as a beacon of inspiration for those around you. Your actions and commitment to pollinator health lead by example, motivating others to embark on their own beekeeping adventures or become advocates for pollinator conservation.

Through your passion, you instill in others a sense of wonder and appreciation for the world of bees. You awaken a reverence for nature and a sense of responsibility for its preservation. Your beekeeping legacy is a testament to the profound.

Chapter BONUS: Introduction to DIY Beehive Construction

Section 1 - Safety First

Safety should always be your paramount concern when embarking on any DIY project, and constructing a beehive is no exception. Beekeeping involves handling tools, materials, and, of course, the bees themselves, which can pose potential risks. By taking the necessary precautions, you'll ensure not only your well-being but also the successful completion of your beehive.

Protective Gear:

Start by equipping yourself with the right protective gear. Safety goggles should always shield your eyes from flying wood splinters, nails, or any debris that may arise during construction. Sturdy work gloves are crucial for safeguarding your hands while handling lumber and working with tools. Depending on your workspace and the materials used, a dust mask may be necessary to protect your respiratory health. Be prepared to switch to a mask if you encounter substantial dust during your work.

Workspace Preparation:

Your workspace plays a significant role in ensuring safety. It should be well-ventilated, especially if you're working with paints, stains, or other materials that emit fumes. Proper ventilation keeps the air fresh and reduces exposure to potentially harmful substances. If you're indoors, open windows and doors to facilitate airflow. When working outdoors, ensure you choose a location with good ventilation to prevent the buildup of fumes.

First-Aid Kit:
Accidents can happen even to the most cautious individuals. Having a first-aid kit on hand is a wise precaution. Ensure your kit is stocked with basic supplies like various-sized bandages, antiseptic wipes, adhesive tape, scissors, and disposable gloves. Familiarize yourself with how to use these supplies in case of minor injuries. Having a well-equipped first-aid kit within easy reach can make all the difference in addressing and resolving unexpected issues swiftly.

Tool Safety:
Your tools are your allies in this construction journey, but they should be used responsibly and according to their intended purpose. Always read and follow the manufacturer's instructions for safe usage. Keep your tools in excellent working condition by maintaining sharp blades, properly

adjusted settings, and clean handles. A well-maintained tool not only ensures precise construction but also reduces the risk of accidents caused by tool malfunctions.

By prioritizing safety with the right protective gear, well-ventilated workspaces, first-aid supplies, and responsible tool usage, you're setting the stage for a secure and successful beehive construction project. These precautions are not just for your protection but also for the overall quality of your work. With safety measures in place, you can confidently embark on your DIY beehive construction journey, knowing you've taken the necessary steps to make it a safe and enjoyable experience.

Section 2: Gather Your Materials

Now that we've covered safety precautions in Section 1, let's move on to one of the most critical aspects of building your DIY beehive: gathering the right materials. Your choice of materials will significantly impact the durability and functionality of your beehive, so it's crucial to select them carefully. In this section, we'll guide you through the materials you'll need for constructing a Langstroth hive, one of the most popular hive designs among beekeepers.

1. Lumber Selection: The backbone of your beehive is the lumber you choose. The most common woods used for beehive construction are pine and cedar, thanks to their durability, resistance to decay, and cost-effectiveness. Here's a breakdown of your lumber needs:

- **Hive Bodies:** For Langstroth hives, hive bodies are typically available in two depths: deep and medium. You'll need lumber boards that are at least 1-inch thick for these components. A typical deep hive body measures 9⅝ inches in height, while a medium one is around 6⅝ inches.

- **Frames:** Frames are crucial for supporting the honeycomb structures that bees build. They are typically made from ¾-inch-thick lumber. The number of frames you'll need depends on the size of your hive bodies, but a Langstroth hive often accommodates 10 frames per hive body.

- **Bottom Board:** The bottom board serves as the hive's base. You'll need lumber boards, typically 1 inch thick, for this component. A standard bottom board measures 22 inches in length and 16⅛ inches in width.

- **Inner and Outer Covers:** Both the inner and outer covers protect the hive from the elements. These components can be made from ½-inch-thick lumber. The dimensions for these covers vary, but a typical Langstroth hive cover measures 19⅞ inches by 16¼ inches.

2. Hive Plans:

Before purchasing your lumber, obtain detailed hive plans that match your chosen hive design, such as Langstroth. Hive plans serve as your blueprint for cutting and assembling the lumber correctly. They provide precise measurements and guidance on how the components fit together. You can find hive plans in beekeeping books, online resources, or from local beekeeping associations.

3. Essential Tools:

To transform your lumber into hive components, gather the following essential tools:

- **Saw:** A saw, such as a circular saw or table saw, is necessary for cutting lumber to the correct dimensions. Ensure your saw's blade is sharp and suitable for cutting wood cleanly.
- **Hammer:** A claw hammer is vital for driving nails and securing hive components. Choose one that feels comfortable in your hand for extended use.
- **Nails and Screws:** You'll need nails for fastening frames together and screws for securing hive components like the bottom board and covers. Choose corrosion-resistant fasteners to ensure the longevity of your hive.
- **Measuring Tape:** Precision is key in beehive construction, so a measuring tape is invaluable for accurately measuring and marking your lumber.
- **Carpenter's Square:** A carpenter's square helps maintain right angles, ensuring that your hive components fit together perfectly.

With the right materials and tools in hand, you're well-prepared to embark on your beehive-building adventure. Take the time to source high-quality lumber, review your hive plans, and ensure your tools are in optimal working condition. By doing so, you'll set the stage for constructing a beehive that not only meets your beekeeping needs but also stands the test of time.

4. Safety Gear Revisited:

As we dive into the construction process, it's essential to revisit safety gear. Make sure you have your safety goggles, gloves, and dust mask ready. These items are your frontline protection against potential hazards during construction. Always prioritize safety to ensure a smooth and secure building experience.

5. Gathering Materials Ethically:

When sourcing your lumber, consider the environmental impact of your choices. Sustainable practices are crucial in beekeeping, and this extends to the materials you use. Look for lumber that is sustainably sourced and certified by organizations like the Forest Stewardship Council (FSC). By choosing responsibly harvested wood, you contribute to the well-being of both your bee colony and the environment.

6. Cost Considerations:

Finally, be mindful of your budget. Building your beehive can be cost-effective, but it's essential to plan your expenses. Compare prices, consider purchasing materials in bulk to save money, and prioritize quality over quantity. While it's tempting to cut corners, investing in high-quality materials will pay off in the long run with a hive that lasts and supports healthy bee colonies. In the upcoming chapters, we'll delve deeper into the step-by-step construction process, where you'll put these materials and tools to use, transforming them into a functional and thriving beehive.

Section 3 - Choose Your Hive Design

Now that you've gathered your materials and are equipped with the necessary safety gear, it's time to make a significant decision: choosing the hive design that best suits your needs. While there are various hive designs to explore, we'll focus on one of the most popular and versatile options—the Langstroth hive. Understanding hive designs is essential because it influences how you'll construct your beehive and manage your bee colonies.

Why Choose the Langstroth Hive Design:

The Langstroth hive is a favorite among beekeepers for several compelling reasons, especially for beginners. Let's delve into what makes this design stand out:

1. **Modularity:** The Langstroth hive's modular structure allows beekeepers to expand or shrink the hive according to colony strength and honey production. This flexibility is advantageous because it adapts to the evolving needs of your bee colony.
2. **Ease of Management:** Managing a Langstroth hive is relatively straightforward, making it an excellent choice for newcomers to beekeeping. The hive's standardized frame size promotes compatibility, simplifying inspections and hive maintenance.

3. **Honey Extraction:** Langstroth hives are designed for efficient honey extraction. The frames can be easily removed and replaced, allowing beekeepers to access honeycombs without disturbing the entire colony.
4. **Widely Adopted:** The Langstroth hive is one of the most commonly used designs worldwide. This means that you'll find ample resources, support, and equipment designed specifically for this hive style. Additionally, if you ever decide to expand your beekeeping knowledge or seek advice from other beekeepers, there will likely be more Langstroth beekeepers in your network.

Understanding the Langstroth Hive Components:

Before diving into construction, it's essential to familiarize yourself with the main components of a Langstroth hive:

1. **Hive Bodies:** Hive bodies are the main boxes that house the bee colony. In a Langstroth hive, there are two standard sizes: deep and medium. Deep hive bodies are used for brood rearing, while medium ones are primarily for honey storage.
2. **Frames:** Frames are inserted into the hive bodies and serve as a foundation for bees to build honeycombs. Frames come in standard sizes and are designed to accommodate beeswax foundation sheets, which encourage bees to construct uniform honeycombs.
3. **Bottom Board:** The bottom board serves as the hive's base, providing an entrance for the bees. It also includes an integrated tray for monitoring and managing pests.
4. **Inner Cover:** The inner cover acts as an insulating barrier between the hive bodies and the outer cover. It often includes a central hole to allow for ventilation and a top entrance for the bees.
5. **Outer Cover:** The outer cover protects the hive from the elements, helping to maintain stable temperature and humidity levels inside. It typically has a telescoping design that extends over the sides of the hive to provide extra protection.

Customizing Your Langstroth Hive:

While the Langstroth design offers a standardized structure, there's room for customization based on your preferences and beekeeping goals. Consider the following options:

1. **Paint or Stain:** You can choose to paint or stain your hive for both protection and aesthetics. Light colors reflect sunlight and heat, helping to keep the hive cooler in hot weather.
2. **Hive Stand:** Elevating your hive with a stand can improve ventilation and protect it from pests like ants.
3. **Ventilation:** Some beekeepers opt to add additional ventilation features, such as screened bottom boards or extra holes in the inner cover, to enhance airflow within the hive.
4. **Top Feeders:** If you plan to provide supplementary feeding for your bees, consider incorporating a top feeder into your hive design. This allows you to feed the bees without opening the hive.
5. **Queen Excluder:** A queen excluder is a device placed between the brood chamber and honey supers to prevent the queen from laying eggs in honey storage frames. While optional, it can help keep honeycombs cleaner.
6. **Hive Tool Storage:** Think about incorporating a hive tool holder on the side of your hive for convenience during inspections.

Ultimately, the Langstroth hive's adaptability and widespread use make it an excellent choice for beginners and experienced beekeepers alike. It offers a solid foundation for your beekeeping journey, and by understanding its components and customization options, you can tailor your Langstroth hive to meet your specific needs and preferences.

Chapter BONUS 2: Constructing Hive Bodies

In this chapter, we'll dive into one of the essential components of your beehive—the hive bodies. Hive bodies are the boxes that house your bee colony and serve as their living quarters. Constructing them correctly is crucial to ensuring a healthy and thriving bee colony. So, let's roll up our sleeves and get started on this exciting part of your DIY beehive construction journey.

Section 1 - Understanding Hive Bodies

Before we jump into the construction process, it's essential to understand the role of hive bodies in your beehive. Hive bodies serve as the main living spaces for your bees, and there are two standard sizes you need to be familiar with:

1. **Deep Hive Bodies:** These are larger and are primarily used for brood rearing. Brood rearing is the process where the queen bee lays her eggs, and the worker bees raise the young bees. A healthy bee colony requires a sufficient number of deep hive bodies for brood rearing.
2. **Medium Hive Bodies:** Medium hive bodies are smaller and are mainly used for honey storage. Once the worker bees have filled these with honey, beekeepers can harvest the frames without disturbing the brood chamber. Medium hive bodies are more manageable in terms of weight, making honey extraction more accessible.

Section 2 - Gathering Your Materials

Before you begin constructing hive bodies, make sure you have all the necessary materials and tools ready. Here's what you'll need:

Materials:
1. **Lumber:** Select high-quality lumber, typically pine or cedar, for your hive bodies. The dimensions will depend on whether you're making deep or medium hive bodies. For deep hive bodies, the standard dimensions are approximately 19 7/8 inches (50.5 cm) in length, 16 1/4 inches (41.3 cm) in width, and 9 5/8 inches (24.4 cm) in height. For medium hive bodies, the dimensions are roughly the same except for the height, which is around 6 5/8 inches (16.8 cm).
2. **Wood Glue:** Use waterproof wood glue to ensure the joints of your hive bodies are strong and durable.

3. **Screws or Nails:** You can choose to use screws or nails for assembly. Screws provide a more secure and long-lasting hold, while nails are quicker to work with. If you opt for screws, make sure they're corrosion-resistant.

Tools:
1. **Saw:** You'll need a saw to cut the lumber to the required dimensions. A table saw or circular saw works well for this task.
2. **Measuring Tape:** Accurate measurements are crucial for a well-constructed hive body. A measuring tape will be your best friend during this process.
3. **Carpenter's Square:** A carpenter's square ensures your cuts are at right angles, which is essential for precise assembly.
4. **Clamps:** Clamps will help you hold the pieces together while the glue dries, ensuring a tight fit.
5. **Drill (if using screws):** If you choose screws for assembly, a drill will make the process much more efficient.
6. **Safety Gear:** Don't forget to wear your safety gear, including safety goggles and gloves, to protect yourself during construction.

Section 3 - Hive Body Assembly

Now that you have gathered all the necessary materials and tools, it's time to roll up your sleeves and start constructing your hive bodies. Hive bodies are the core components of your beehive, providing the living space for your bee colony. In this section, we will focus on constructing one deep hive body and one medium hive body, as these are the most commonly used sizes in beekeeping. Let's dive into the step-by-step process of hive body assembly.

Constructing a Deep Hive Body:

Step 1: Cut the Lumber
Start by ensuring you have the right dimensions for your deep hive body. For standard Langstroth hives, the dimensions are approximately 19 7/8 inches (50.5 cm) in length, 16 1/4 inches (41.3 cm) in width, and 9 5/8 inches (24.4 cm) in height. If you are using different dimensions for your specific hive design, make sure to adjust accordingly.

Using your saw, carefully cut the lumber to the required dimensions. It's crucial to make precise cuts to ensure your hive body assembles correctly.

Step 2: Assemble the Sides

Now that you have your cut pieces, it's time to assemble the hive body. Begin with the shorter sides. Apply a thin layer of waterproof wood glue along one of the shorter edges. Make sure the glue is evenly spread to ensure a strong bond.

Take one of the shorter pieces and align it with the glued edge. The edges should be flush. Use clamps to hold the pieces in place while you secure them together. Depending on your preference and the availability of tools, you can use screws or nails for this step. Screws provide a more secure and long-lasting hold, while nails are quicker to work with.

Repeat this step for the other short side, creating a rectangular box. Ensure that the corners are square by using a carpenter's square to check the angles. This step is crucial to maintain the structural integrity of your hive body.

Step 3: Attach the Front and Back
With the shorter sides in place, it's time to attach the longer front and back pieces. Apply wood glue along the edges of the shorter sides that will come into contact with the longer sides. Also, apply glue along one edge of each of the longer sides.
Carefully position the longer sides to create a rectangular box. Make sure the edges are flush and the corners are square. Secure them in place with screws or nails, as per your preference. Again, use clamps to hold everything together while the glue dries.

Step 4: Drill Ventilation Holes (Optional)
While not mandatory, adding ventilation holes to your deep hive body can improve airflow for your bees. Proper ventilation helps regulate the hive's temperature and humidity, contributing to the overall health of your bee colony.
To add ventilation holes, use a drill with a small bit (around 1/4 inch or 0.6 cm). Drill holes in the sides or bottom of the deep hive body. The number and placement of holes depend on your preference, but make sure they are evenly spaced and do not compromise the structural integrity of the hive.

Constructing a Medium Hive Body:

Step 1: Cut the Lumber
Constructing a medium hive body follows the same principles as the deep hive body, with the main difference being the dimensions. For medium hive bodies in a Langstroth hive, the dimensions are approximately the same as the deep hive body, except for the height, which should be around 6 5/8 inches (16.8 cm).

Ensure you have the correct dimensions and cut the lumber accordingly using your saw. As with the deep hive body, precision in your cuts is essential.

Step 2: Follow Assembly Steps
The assembly process for the medium hive body is identical to the deep hive body, with adjustments made for the dimensions. You will assemble the shorter sides first, followed by the longer front and back sides, all while applying wood glue and securing the pieces with screws or nails.

Section 4: Painting or Staining Your Hive Bodies (Optional)
With your hive bodies now constructed, you have the option to paint or stain them. Painting or staining serves both aesthetic and protective purposes. It can help protect the wood from weathering, extend the hive bodies' lifespan, and provide a visually appealing finish.
Here are the steps to consider if you choose to paint or stain your hive bodies:

Step 1: Choose Bee-Friendly Paint or Stain
Select a paint or stain that is safe for bees. Avoid using toxic or lead-based products, as these can harm your bee colony. Look for non-toxic, bee-friendly options available at your local hardware store or beekeeping supply shop.

Step 2: Prepare Your Workspace
Find a well-ventilated area for painting or staining, preferably outdoors or in a well-ventilated garage. Lay down a drop cloth or plastic sheet to protect your work surface.

Step 3: Sand the Hive Bodies (Optional)
If the wood surfaces are rough, you may choose to lightly sand them before applying paint or stain. Sanding can create a smoother finish and allow the paint or stain to adhere better.

Step 4: Apply Paint or Stain
Follow the manufacturer's instructions for your chosen paint or stain. Use a brush, roller, or spray application, depending on your preference and the product's recommendations. Apply an even coat to all external surfaces of the hive bodies, including the sides, front, back, and top.

Step 5: Allow to Dry
Allow the paint or stain to dry thoroughly according to the product's recommended drying time. Ensure the hive bodies are completely dry before placing them in the bee yard.

Step 6: Assemble Your Beehive

Once your painted or stained hive bodies are dry, you can proceed with assembling your complete beehive. In the next chapter, we will focus on the assembly of frames, another critical component for your bee colony.

Congratulations! You've completed the assembly of your hive bodies, and your beehive is taking shape. Stay tuned for Chapter 3, where we'll delve into the construction of frames, providing your bees with spaces to store honey and raise brood. Beekeeping is an exciting journey, and you're well on your way to becoming a successful beekeeper!

Section 4 - Preparing the Work Area

Before you embark on the exciting journey of constructing your beehive, it's essential to prepare your work area adequately. A well-organized and suitable workspace ensures that you can complete your project efficiently and with precision. In this section, we will guide you through the process of creating an ideal work area for beehive construction.

1. Selecting the Right Location

Choosing the right location for your workspace is the first step in preparing for your beehive construction project. Here are some considerations:

- **Indoor vs. Outdoor:** Depending on your circumstances and the season, you can choose to work indoors or outdoors. Indoor spaces offer protection from the elements and may be preferable during inclement weather. However, outdoor spaces provide ample ventilation and natural light.
- **Well-Ventilated:** Whether indoors or outdoors, ensure that the workspace is well-ventilated. Good ventilation helps disperse any fumes or dust created during construction.
- **Level Surface:** It's crucial to work on a level surface. This ensures that your hive components are assembled accurately and that the beehive stands securely once installed.
- **Access to Tools:** Make sure your workspace has easy access to the tools and materials you'll need. This prevents unnecessary trips back and forth and keeps your work organized.

2. Workbench or Sawhorses

Having a dedicated workbench or a set of sturdy sawhorses is highly recommended. These provide a stable and elevated surface to work on, making it easier to assemble hive components.

If you're working indoors, a workbench is particularly useful. Outdoors, sawhorses can be set up on a flat, level surface.

3. Organizing Materials

Before you begin construction, organize all the materials you'll need. This includes lumber, tools, safety gear, and any other supplies. Having everything within reach prevents interruptions and keeps the workflow smooth.

4. Safety Considerations

Safety should remain a priority throughout the construction process. Here are some safety considerations for your workspace:

- **Safety Gear:** Ensure you have all the necessary safety gear on hand. This includes safety goggles, gloves, a dust mask, and any other protective equipment suitable for the task.
- **First-Aid Kit:** Accidents can happen, so having a first-aid kit readily available is essential. Be sure it's well-stocked and accessible.
- **Fire Safety:** If you're working in an indoor workspace, be mindful of fire safety. Keep flammable materials away from potential sources of ignition and have a fire extinguisher on hand.
- **Ventilation:** Adequate ventilation prevents the buildup of fumes from adhesives, paints, or other materials you may use. Ensure that windows and doors can be opened to allow fresh air circulation.

5. Proper Lighting

Good lighting is crucial for accurate assembly and for your safety. Ensure that your workspace is well-lit, especially if you plan to work indoors or during the evening hours. Natural light is ideal, but if that's not possible, invest in bright, adjustable work lights.

6. Organization and Cleanliness

An organized and clean workspace contributes to an efficient workflow. Keep your tools and materials organized, and clean up as you go. This prevents accidents and ensures that you can find what you need when you need it.

7. Seating and Comfort

You'll spend a significant amount of time in your workspace, so consider your comfort. If you're using a workbench or sawhorses, invest in a comfortable chair or stool. Adequate seating ensures that you can work with precision without discomfort.

8. Clear Work Surface

Keep your work surface clear of clutter and unnecessary items. This minimizes distractions and allows you to focus on hive construction. Create dedicated spaces for tools and materials, and put everything back in its place after use.

9. Setting Realistic Expectations

Lastly, set realistic expectations for your work area. Consider the size and scope of your project and ensure that your workspace can comfortably accommodate it. If you need additional space or support, don't hesitate to make the necessary adjustments.

By following these steps and adequately preparing your work area, you'll create an environment conducive to efficient and safe beehive construction. Once your workspace is ready, you can confidently move on to the next chapter, where we'll delve into the specifics of hive components and their assembly. With everything in place, you're well on your way to constructing your DIY beehive successfully.

Section 5 - Understanding Hive Components

Understanding the various components of your beehive is crucial for effective beekeeping. In this section, we will explore the essential hive components in detail, explaining their functions and how they contribute to the overall well-being of your bee colony.

1. Hive Bodies

Hive bodies, also known as hive boxes, are the main structural components of a beehive. They come in different sizes, with the two most common being deep and medium hive bodies. Here's what you need to know about them:

- **Deep Hive Body**: This larger-sized box serves as the brood chamber, where the queen bee lays her eggs, and worker bees raise brood (young bees). The deep hive body is typically placed at the bottom of the hive stack.
- **Medium Hive Body**: The medium-sized box, also known as a honey super, is where bees store surplus honey. Beekeepers often use one or more medium hive bodies above the deep hive body for honey storage.

2. Frames

Frames are rectangular structures that fit inside the hive bodies and serve as the foundation for honeycomb construction. Bees use frames to build their wax comb, where they store honey, pollen, and raise brood. Frames are essential for maintaining hive structure and facilitating easy inspection. They come in various sizes, such as deep frames for brood chambers and medium frames for honey supers.

3. Bottom Board

The bottom board is the base of your beehive. It provides stability to the hive and serves as the landing and take-off platform for bees. Properly ventilated bottom boards help regulate the hive's temperature and humidity. Some bottom boards have screened sections that assist in ventilation and also aid in monitoring for pests like Varroa mites.

4. Inner Cover

The inner cover is a component placed directly under the outer cover. It provides insulation and ventilation to the hive while protecting the bees from extreme weather conditions. The inner cover typically features a central hole or notch for ventilation, allowing bees to control the hive's temperature and humidity.

5. Outer Cover

The outer cover is the topmost component of the beehive. It shields the hive from rain, wind, and other environmental elements, helping to maintain the hive's internal climate. Outer covers come in various styles, including telescoping covers and migratory covers. Properly securing the outer cover ensures the hive's protection.

6. Queen Excluder (Optional)

A queen excluder is a grid-like component placed between the hive body and honey supers. It is designed to prevent the queen bee from accessing the honey supers, where surplus honey is stored. This separation ensures that brood rearing occurs exclusively in the deep hive body, keeping honey frames free from brood. Not all beekeepers use queen excluders, but they can be valuable in specific beekeeping practices.

7. Hive Stand

While not part of the hive stack, the hive stand is an essential component. It elevates the hive off the ground, providing stability and protection from dampness. Elevating the hive also makes it less accessible to pests like ants and rodents.

Understanding these hive components is fundamental for effective hive management. Proper use and placement of these components contribute to the health and productivity of your bee colony.

As you progress in your beekeeping journey, you may encounter variations and additional components, depending on hive designs and beekeeping practices.

CONCLUSION

Congratulations on reaching the conclusion of this comprehensive step-by-step guide to building your own beehive! Throughout this journey, you've gained valuable knowledge, learned essential skills, and embarked on an exciting adventure into the world of beekeeping. As we wrap up, let's take a moment to reflect on your accomplishments and the next steps in your beekeeping journey.

Celebrating Your Achievement
Building your beehive from scratch is a remarkable feat. You've demonstrated dedication, patience, and a commitment to the well-being of your future bee colonies. The beehive you've constructed is not just a wooden structure; it's a home for your bees, a testament to your craftsmanship, and a symbol of your dedication to sustainable beekeeping.

The Path Ahead
As you stand before your completed beehive, you're likely filled with anticipation and excitement about the beekeeping adventures to come. Here are some essential steps to consider as you move forward:

1. **Hive Placement:** Carefully choose the location for your beehive. Ensure it receives ample sunlight, is sheltered from strong winds, and is easily accessible for your routine inspections.
2. **Obtain Bees:** Acquire a bee colony, which typically comes in the form of a package of bees or a nucleus colony (nuc). Research local bee suppliers or beekeeping clubs for the best options.
3. **Hive Maintenance:** Regularly inspect and maintain your beehive to ensure the health and productivity of your bee colony. This includes monitoring for pests, diseases, and providing necessary care.
4. **Harvesting Honey:** As your bee colony thrives, you'll have the opportunity to harvest honey, beeswax, and other hive products. Learn about the best practices for ethical and sustainable harvesting.
5. **Expand Your Knowledge:** Beekeeping is a continuous learning experience. Stay informed about the latest developments in beekeeping practices, attend beekeeping workshops or join local beekeeping associations, and connect with experienced beekeepers.
6. **Bee-Friendly Landscaping:** Consider planting bee-friendly flowers and plants around your hive to provide a diverse foraging environment for your bees and support local pollinators.

The Joy of Beekeeping

Beekeeping is not just a hobby; it's a fulfilling and rewarding journey. It connects you with the natural world, fosters a deeper appreciation for these remarkable creatures, and contributes to the essential role bees play in pollination and ecosystem health.

As you embark on this new chapter of beekeeping, remember to be patient and observant. Each hive has its unique dynamics, and by closely monitoring your bees, you'll become attuned to their needs and behaviors. Your beehive will thrive under your attentive care.

Sharing Your Knowledge

Just as you've benefitted from this guide, consider sharing your knowledge and experiences with others. Mentor aspiring beekeepers, engage in local beekeeping communities, and advocate for pollinator conservation. By doing so, you'll not only contribute to the well-being of bees but also inspire others to embark on their own beekeeping adventures.

A Bright Beekeeping Future

Your DIY beehive construction journey is just the beginning of a fulfilling and lifelong engagement with bees and beekeeping. With the hive you've built and the knowledge you've acquired, you're well-prepared to nurture and protect your bee colony. Remember that beekeeping is a journey of learning and discovery, and your commitment to responsible beekeeping practices will make a positive impact on both your local community and the broader ecosystem.

As you move forward, may your beekeeping endeavors be filled with wonder, joy, and the sweet rewards of nature. Thank you for choosing this guide as your companion on your beekeeping journey. Wishing you success, fulfillment, and a thriving beehive teeming with the diligent buzz of your beloved bees.

Glossary

Beehive: A structure where bees live and store honey.

Brood: The developing young bees, including eggs, larvae, and pupae, found in the brood chamber or deep hive body.

Brood Chamber: The section of the hive where the queen bee lays eggs, and worker bees raise brood.

Frames: Rectangular structures that hold honeycomb.

Honey Super: A hive body placed above the brood chamber to collect surplus honey.

Hive Body: The main structural component of a beehive, available in deep and medium sizes.

Inner Cover: A component placed below the outer cover to provide insulation and ventilation while protecting the bees.

Outer Cover: The topmost component of the beehive, protecting it from environmental elements.

Queen Bee: The female bee responsible for laying eggs and maintaining the colony's reproductive cycle.

Queen Excluder: An optional grid-like component placed between the brood chamber and honey supers to prevent the queen from accessing honey storage areas.

Bottom Board: The base of the beehive, providing stability and a landing platform for bees.

Hive Stand: A structure that elevates the beehive off the ground, providing stability and protection from dampness and pests.

Varroa Mites: Parasitic mites that can infest bee colonies and weaken bee populations.

Telescoping Cover: An outer cover with edges that extend over the sides of the hive, providing extra protection.

Migratory Cover: An outer cover that fits flush with the sides of the hive, providing a sleek, low-profile design.

Screened Bottom Board: A bottom board with a screened section, aiding in ventilation and pest monitoring.

Medium Frames: Frames of intermediate size, commonly used in honey supers for honey storage.

Deep Frames: Larger frames typically used in the brood chamber for raising brood and storing honey and pollen.

Brood Rearing: The process by which worker bees raise and care for the developing brood, including eggs, larvae, and pupae.

Honeycomb: A waxy structure built by bees to store honey, pollen, and provide cells for brood rearing.

Honey Harvesting: The process of collecting surplus honey from the beehive for human consumption.

Ventilation: The process of allowing air to flow through the hive, regulating temperature and humidity.

Pollen: Small grains collected by bees from flowers and used as a protein source in the hive.

First Aid Supplies: Medical items kept on hand for treating minor injuries or bee stings during beekeeping activities.

Safety Gear: Protective equipment such as gloves, safety goggles, and dust masks to ensure the safety of beekeepers.

Hive Plans: Detailed diagrams and instructions for building beehives, helping beekeepers create structurally sound hives.

Hive Stack: The arrangement of hive bodies, frames, and other hive components within a beehive.

Hive Management: The practices and strategies employed by beekeepers to care for bee colonies, including inspections, feeding, and disease control.

Queen Rearing: A process in which beekeepers intentionally raise queen bees to replace aging or failing queens or to create nucleus colonies.

Nucleus Colony: A small, self-contained bee colony created from a larger hive, typically containing a queen, workers, and brood.

Swarming: A natural process in which a portion of the bee colony leaves with the old queen to establish a new hive.

Supers: Additional hive bodies placed above the brood chamber for honey storage.

Bee Space: The optimal gap or space between frames and hive components that allows bees to move freely without building excess comb or feeling threatened.

Bee Bread: A mixture of pollen, nectar, and bee secretions used as a food source for young bees.

Beekeeping: The practice of maintaining bee colonies for various purposes, including honey production, pollination, and environmental conservation.

Hive Tool: A specialized tool used by beekeepers to pry apart hive components, remove frames, and scrape excess wax and propolis.

Propolis: A resinous substance collected by bees from tree buds and used to seal cracks and crevices within the hive.

Langstroth Hive: A widely used beehive design characterized by removable frames, making hive inspections and honey extraction easier.

Wood Glue: An adhesive used in beehive assembly to bond wooden components together securely.

This glossary provides essential terms and definitions relevant to beekeeping and beehive construction, aiding beekeepers in understanding the terminology used throughout this guide.

Printed in Great Britain
by Amazon